Guidelines
and Games
for
Teaching Efficient
Braille Reading

Guidelines and Games for Teaching Efficient Braille Reading

Myrna R. Olson, Ed.D.
Associate Professor & Chairperson
Department of Special Education
University of North Dakota

In collaboration with
Sally S. Mangold, Ph.D.
Assistant Professor
Special Education Department
San Francisco State University

PRESS
NEW YORK

Guidelines and Games for Teaching Efficient Braille Reading
is © 1981 by: American Foundation for the Blind
11 Penn Plaza, Suite 300
New York, NY 10001

ISBN: 0-89128-105-3

Library of Congress Cataloging in Publication Data

Olson, Myrna R.
   Guidelines and games for teaching efficient braille reading.

   Bibliography: p.
   1. Blind—Education—Reading. 2. Children, Blind—Education. 3. Educational games
1. Mangold, Sally S.   II. American Foundation for the Blind.   III. Title.   IV. Title: Braille reading.
HV1669.042   37191'14   81-14906
ISBN 0-89128-105-3   AACR2

Reprinted 1996

Printed in United States of America

Contents

Preface

Braille has been upheld as a worthwhile mode of reading for visually handicapped persons since its invention. It affords the reader several advantages over auditory reading modes—a form of independence, a means of note-taking, a way of learning spelling and punctuation, and an opportunity to review material that has been read previously. Its bulkiness and high cost are definite drawbacks, but the overriding disadvantage of braille is the length of time consumed in tactually reading it. The average speed of braille readers falls progressively behind the average speed of print readers as they move through the grades. Adult braille readers consequently read much more slowly than their seeing counterparts.

In 1969, Lowenfeld, Abel, and Hatlen reported an extensive study on the status of braille reading in public and residential schools. Some discussion of the challenge involved in teaching braille reading was included in their book. Now, years later, beginning teachers have but one textbook that provides actual guidelines for teaching braille reading (Harley, Henderson, & Truan, 1979).

Most of my five years as a residential school teacher of the visually handicapped were spent working with children who had already been taught to read braille. I was frustrated by the rate at which my students read as well as by their various bad mechanical habits. In 1974 I began training teachers in the area of visual impairment at the University of North Dakota. Conducting research for my dissertation at that time, I became interested in the writings of Dr. Vearl McBride of Culver-Stockton College, Canton, Missouri. An article appearing in the *New Outlook for the Blind* reported reading rate gains over 400% for braille readers after a two-week workshop conducted by McBride. Comprehension levels for these readers were said to have dropped slightly, but no standardized test was given to measure that amount.

In August 1974 I received permission to administer a standardized test to the braille reading participants in one of Dr. McBride's workshops. The reading rate gains on this test were much more modest (30-35%) than those recorded through informal testing (200 + %). Comprehension levels did, however, remain stable at a satisfactory level (80 + %). Following that workshop I taught a workshop of my own based upon McBride's procedures, and obtained results that were not significantly different from McBride's. One of the more interesting conclusions of my research was the negative correlation I found between age and percent increase in reading rate achieved by participants in both workshops. It seems that the longer one has been entrenched in bad reading habits, the more difficult it is to break those habits. During an informal follow-up, I also discovered that few workshop participants maintained their gains in reading rate.

It became clear to me that rather than attempt "remedial" instruction with adult readers, it would be better to teach braille incorporating rapid reading principles from the readiness level of reading on up. I considered writing a book at that time, but felt a need for information and feedback from someone who had taught more beginning braille reading than I had. This need was met during the summer of 1977, when I met Dr. Sally Mangold at a summer session at San Francisco State University. She had been a resource teacher of the visually handicapped for 15 years and had just completed her doctoral study on the topic of braille reading. She had discovered through her doctoral study the advantage of concentrating on the development of good mechanical skills during beginning braille instruction.

Over the past year, Sally and I have managed to collaborate on this book by means of long distance phone calls and while attending the same conventions across the country. Sally's background in reading-related research and long experience as a resource teacher, coupled with the fact that she is a braille user herself, made her contributions to the first five chapters extremely valuable. In addition, she wrote Chapter Six on games and activities for adding "spice" to a braille reading program. We believe that our book offers something unique. It provides parents, vision teachers, and regular classroom teachers with ideas for adapting a general reading program to the needs of braille readers. Activities and games offered provide enrichment to the traditional teaching of braille reading skills from the pre-school level through grade three. Suggestions for working with remedial readers, regardless of their ages, are also provided.

Myrna R. Olson, Ed.D.
Associate Professor of Special Education
University of North Dakota

Guidelines
and Games
for
Teaching Efficient
Braille Reading

Chapter I
Introduction

Audience/Intent

This book on braille reading is intended for parents, pre-school workers, resource/itinerant teachers, vision consultants, and teacher educators. Many of the ideas presented will also be helpful to regular classroom teachers who have braille readers in a mainstreamed setting. Public Law 94-142, mandating equal educational rights for all handicapped children will no doubt have an impact on the number of blind children being served in public schools. Regardless of whether or not they receive outside help with these children, regular classroom teachers will need to know as much as possible about the braille reading system.

Assumptions

It is assumed that anyone teaching a child to read braille has the following competencies:

Knowledge of Braille Code

Any individual planning to introduce braille to another person must have adequate knowledge of the braille reading code. This is important for deciding a sequence for the introduction of contractions and analyzing the student's reading errors.

If a formal course on braille is unavailable in one's local community, one can obtain self-instructional materials from two sources: (1) The Library of Congress, National Library Service for the Blind and Physically Handicapped, distributes free self-instructional manuals for learning to transcribe braille. A set of braille drills accompanies the manual so that one can correct a portion of one's own work. A manuscript at the end of the manual may also be submitted to the Library of Congress for their inspection. It is checked for errors and returned with a certificate of satisfactory completion if no errors are found. The following two manuals should be requested when writing to the Library of Congress:

Dorf, M. and Scharry, E. *Instruction manual for braille transcribing.* Washington, D.C.: Library of Congress, 1973.
Dorf, M. and Scharry, E. *Supplement: Drills reproduced in braille.* Washington, D.C.: Library of Congress, 1971.

(2) As an alternative to the correspondence arrangement provided by the Library of Congress, the prospective learner of braille may find another self-instructional text helpful:

Ashcroft, S. and Henderson, F. *Programmed instruction in braille.* Pittsburgh, Pennsylvania: Stanwix House Incorporated, 1963. It is written in a programmed text format with inkprint versions of the braille lessons provided for self-checking.

Whichever self-instructional text a person chooses, access to a braille writing machine will be necessary. Most public libraries and/or college libraries have these machines available for use. The cost of buying one's own braille writer may be prohibitive ($100-250). Slates and styluses are much less expensive ($1-20), but to use them, the braillist must punch out single braille dots one by one in a mirror image fashion. Slates come in all sizes (pocket to desk size) and are made of a variety of materials (nickel, gold, plastic). One of the best slates has a drop-out window that permits "proof-reading" of one's braille with the frame still clamped to the paper. In the past many blind individuals were taught to write braille with a slate and stylus from the beginning; current trends in teaching postpone its introduction as a writing tool until the braille code has been mastered. All types of writing devices are available from the American Printing House for the Blind, 1839 Frankfort Avenue, Louisville, Kentucky 40206.

Understanding the Major Reading Methods

It would be wonderful if all children could learn to read in the same manner. In fact, children learn the skill in very different ways, depending upon their in-born abilities, their experiences, and their motivation and interests. For this reason, every teacher must have knowledge of the major methods for teaching reading. A bibliography of textbooks is provided at the end of this chapter for anyone wishing to "brush up" on general methods for teaching reading. What follows is a brief description of those methods I feel one should be able to use in conjunction with this text.

1) *Basal System.* To use most basal reading series implies a five-step method. Vocabulary is usually introduced through a pre-reading discussion of the story. This is followed by silent reading, during which the story is ready part by part with pre-reading and post-reading questions and discussion. It has become the practice to urge children to attack new words for themselves, using techniques they have been taught. Oral reading is now being emphasized as a follow-up to silent reading. It is used to promote depth of interpretation of silent reading. These activities are often followed by skill-building exercises based upon the workbook, commercial or teacher-made kits and vocabulary games or word analysis. It is common for pupils to be grouped according to their reading ability. The basal reading series of the last half century have employed word attack skills (phonics, structural analysis, and contextual analysis) rather than the whole word approach to word recognition. In recent years, the final step in using a basal reading approach has been

to provide supplementary materials. This might include other library books, listening materials, or stories children have dictated themselves.

2) *Phonic Approaches.* Phonic systems emphasize the sounds of letters and are usually one of two types. The analytic approach teaches letter sounds as integral parts of words, after a number of words have been learned. In the synthetic approach, isolated letter sounds are stressed before any experience with words. Phonic systems vary greatly in that some teach vowel sounds before consonant sounds, others reverse the sequence. Phonics enables the child to pronounce and recognize only those words that are aurally familiar to him.

3) *Language Experience Approach.* Proponents of the language experience approach base learning to read upon the child's classroom and out-of-school experiences. These experiences are supplemented by audio-visual materials, pictures, and oral discussion. Children are encouraged to write about them and subsequently read what they have written. The program proceeds from small group oral composition, written down by the teacher, to individualized or interest group composition, written down by the children. Vocabulary skills, writing mechanics, handwriting and phonics skills are promoted through repeated use of the children's own materials.

4) *Linguistic Approach.* There is no such thing as the linguistic method of teaching reading. Rather, a group of ideas gathered from various schools of linguistics has developed into sets of instructional materials. Most linguists believe that beginning texts should include only regularly spelled words or those having consistent grapheme-phoneme correspondence, i.e., the way the words are written tells how to pronounce them. Children are taught to emphasize the sound-symbol relationship rather than clues to word recognition. Phonics is eliminated on the basis that it teaches children to sound words they already know or that letters make sounds. Linguists also emphasize learning of syntax and sentence patterns to aid comprehension. They further hold that reading should be largely oral and depend upon auditory memory of language. Reading and writing are looked upon as secondary to speech and derived from oral language.

5) *Individualized Reading Approaches.* Individualized reading involves grouping for many activities and assigning reading for both individuals and groups. Basal reading materials and small group reading from identical texts are not abandoned altogether with this approach. Individualized reading often begins with teacher directions to the class as a whole. A period is devoted to independent reading of self-selected material. The teacher often holds teacher-child conferences apart from the class, teacher-child conferences with successive members of a group, or teacher-group conferences. Students' reading levels are assessed continually during this time. These conferences may also include oral reading, exploration of feelings toward the material read, planning for follow-up activities, and drill work. There is usually an attempt to arrange groupings for skill needs, special interests, and social purposes.

Ability to Select and Adapt Reading Approaches

Some children are extremely poor in the areas of auditory memory and auditory discrimination. The wise teacher does not force such children to read through a rigid phonics approach, because the demands on auditory processing are too great. Instead, she might select an approach that relies more heavily on tactual memory.

Whatever a particular child's strengths or weaknesses, the teacher must be able to adapt her "favorite approach" to his needs.

Ability to Obtain Resources

Most school districts have less funding than is needed for purchasing braille materials and transcriber assistance. A competent vision teacher searches out organizations to make donations and supply volunteers for transcribing braille materials. This search may involve speaking to volunteer organizations and helping individuals get started with a correspondence course on braille through the Library of Congress.

Knowledge of the Unique Aspects Involved in Teaching Braille Reading

Braille reading resembles print reading in many ways. There are, however, important differences in the two mediums. This book has been organized into six chapters that will, we hope, make teachers more aware of the uniquenesses of teaching braille reading.

Organization and Content of This Book

The remaining pages of this chapter will be devoted to a synopsis of this book by individual chapter. The reader will note that throughout each chapter the male gender has been used when referring to the student and the female gender used in reference to the teacher. There is no bias or discrimination implied by this practice. Rather than list double gender for every pronoun used (he/she, him/her), I made this arbitrary decision for the sake of brevity.

Chapter One — Introduction

The present chapter describes the rationale and assumptions upon which the entire book was written. It is intended to provide the reader with a quick overview of each chapter.

Chapter Two — Background on Braille Reading

The history of braille reading is interpreted broadly to include a discussion of its development, nature, and use. The advantages of braille over other non-print reading modes are discussed, followed by a summary of the basic perceptual nature of braille reading as compared to print reading. The latter portion of this chapter is devoted to a review of the literature relating to the braille reading habits of children and the common approaches to teaching braille.

Chapter Three — Pre-School Experiences Important to Braille Reading Readiness

Specific suggestions are offered to parents, teachers, and pre-school workers for providing pertinent pre-braille experiences to young children. The unique needs of blind children are addressed within the framework of sensory-motor development, concept development, and reading awareness.

Chapter Four — Activities for Teaching Braille More Efficiently at the Beginning Level

This chapter suggests numerous activities to use with braille readers in the skill areas listed below. Most of the activities are geared to make braille reading a more efficient process by incorporating rapid reading principles into beginning braille instruction.

Skill Areas:
1) Attitude Development
2) Mechanical Skills
3) Hand Movements/Finger Positions
4) Light Finger Touch
5) Tactile Perception/Discrimination
6) Comprehension Skills
7) Flexibility Skills
8) Reading Style Development
9) Memorization of the Braille Code Rules

The final section of this chapter suggests various ways of facilitating carry-over of braille skills learned in a special setting to the regular classroom.

Chapter Five — Ideas for Working with Problem Readers

Specific suggestions for working with various types of problem readers are given. The first part of the chapter identifies the problems of the "remedial reader" in general. Prescriptions are given for working on problems falling into 14 different skill areas. The latter portion of the chapter is devoted to special considerations that must be given to remedial readers who are former print readers.

Chapter Six — Adding Spice to Braille Reading Program Activities

The activities and games outlined in this chapter are appropriate for pre-school, kindergarten, and first- through third-grade-level readers, regardless of their chronological ages. It is hoped that they will help to maintain high motivation toward learning to read, while reinforcing the skills that have been introduced.

Books on Methods of Teaching Beginning Reading

Anderson, V. *Reading and young children.* New York: Macmillan, 1968.
Bammen, H., Dawson, M. & McGovern, J. *Fundamentals of basic reading instruction.* New York: David McKay, 1973.

Bush, C., & Huebner, M. *Strategies for reading in the elementary school.* New York: Macmillan, 1970.

Duffy, G,. & Sherman, G. *Systematic reading instruction.* New York: Harper and Row, 1972.

Durr, W. *Reading instruction: Dimensions and issues.* Boston: Houghton Mifflin, 1967.

Durkin, D. *Teaching young children to read.* Rockleigh, N.J.: Allyn and Bacon, 1972.

Hafner, L. & Hayden, B. *Patterns of teaching reading in the elementary school.* New York: Macmillan, 1972.

Harley, R., Henderson F., & Truan, M. *The teaching of braille reading.* Springfield, Ill.: Charles C Thomas, 1979.

Harris, A. *Effective teaching of reading.* New York: David McKay, 1962.

Harris, L., & Smith, C. *Reading instruction through diagnostic teaching.* New York: Holt, Rinehart, and Winston, 1972.

Karlin, R. *Teaching elementary reading—principles and strategies.* New York: Harcourt, Brace, Jovanovich, 1971.

Miller, W. *Elementary reading today.* New York: Holt, Rinehart, and Winston, 1972.

Ruddell, R. *Reading-language instruction: Innovative practices.* Englewood Cliffs, N.J.: Prentice-Hall, 1973.

Smith, J. *Setting conditions for the creative teaching of reading and literature in the elementary school.* Rockleigh, N.J.: Allyn and Bacon, 1967.

Spache, G. *Reading in the elementary school.* Rockleigh, N.J.: Allyn and Bacon, 1964.

Spache, G. *The teaching of reading, methods and results: An overview.* Bloomington, Ind.: Phi Delta Kappa, 1972.

Spache, G. *Reading in the elementary school.* Rockleigh, N.J.: Allyn and Bacon, 1977.

Stauffner, R. *Teaching reading as a thinking process.* New York: Harper and Row, 1969.

Strang, R. *Diagnostic teaching of reading.* (2nd Ed.). Hightstown, N.J.: McGraw-Hill, 1969.

Veach, J. *Reading in the elementary school.* New York: Ronald Press, 1966.

Chapter II
Background on Braille Reading

Development of a Standardized Braille Code

The tactile system of reading that we know as braille came into being over a long period of time. The first tactually perceptible code was developed in the early nineteenth century by Charles Barbier, a French army officer. His code enabled his men to send and receive messages at night. Louis Braille learned Barbier's system, but found it had serious drawbacks. Still only 15 years old, he decided to work out his own method, and, by 1824 had come up with a reading system using embossed dots. Its official adoption by the Royal Institution for Blind Youth, where Braille was a student, was not, however, until much later. In 1869, the Missouri School for the Blind became the first institution in the United States to adopt the code.

For decades, the advantages and disadvantages of the new system were argued by educators of the visually handicapped. Not until 1932 did the United States finally reach agreement with England to accept English braille (Grade I) as a standard form for embossing. The American Printing House for the Blind modified the 1932 code in 1959. In an attempt to keep the literary code concurrent with innovations and formats being used in print, further minor revisions were made in 1962, 1966 and 1968.

The official code, *Standard English Braille*, consists of alphabet letters, numbers, punctuation, composition signs, 189 contractions, and short form words. The braille cell consists of two vertical rows of three dots each.

Many investigators have concerned themselves with establishing optimal dot size, dot configurations, and spacing among dots. The official spacing used today was reported to be mutually beneficial for children and adults. It provides .09 in. between dot centers, both vertically and horizontally within a cell. Between cells, the spacing is .16 in. and the dot height .025 in., or less.

Future of Braille

Braille reading and writing will most probably remain the major means of communication for individuals who are seriously visually impaired. As Nolan (1979) points out, braille is the only medium in which the blind can write and at the same time read. Despite the easy access to print that recorded books and magazines give blind persons, Mellor (1979) notes the following uses of braille which are unsurpassed by other mediums: (1) providing random access to any page; (2) skimming a page; (3) labelling; (4) filing; (5) writing memoranda; (6) reading tables and diagrams; (7) reading technical or difficult material; (8) demanding the reader to be an active participant rather than a passive listener; and (10) providing deafblind persons their sole means of reading. It is essential, therefore, that we continue to improve the way braille is read, written, stored and produced.

Innovations in Braille Reading, Writing and Production

Braille Without Paper

There are a number of devices, at or near marketing stage, which store information on audio cassette tapes and present it in braille form on displays ranging from 12 to 32 braille cells in length. The braille dots in these cells are formed by six pins the same size as braille dots. The information gets on the tape by the operation of a keyboard much like that of a regular braille writer. Instead of embossing the braille on paper, it is converted to a digital code that is recorded on the tape in a cassette. The encoded information then moves the 6 pins up and down in each braille cell to make the appropriate configurations on the display. To read, the user runs his fingers over the cells and at the end of the line touches a switch which instantly changes the arrangement of all the pins so that the next line stored on the tape is formed.

These devices store from 300-520 pages of braille on a single cassette tape. They vary in complexity in that some combine audio capability with that for braille and at least one has sophisticated indexing and place-finding capability. One machine is desk-top portable, while the others are portable. All of these machines are quiet in operation, which is an advantage for note-taking during meetings and lectures. Most of them can be coupled to typewriters, calculators and computers. At present, costs range from approximately $2,400 to $6,000 (Mellor, 1979; Nolan, 1979).

The advantages of paperless braille machines are numerous. There is a tremendous reduction in the storage space needed for braille materials; students can conveniently carry braille books and assignments to and from school. The information handling features of some of these machines will permit blind students flexibility in writing assignments, editing and correcting mistakes, and filing notes in cassette notebooks for rapid machine retrieval. There is potential for reducing the time required for producing braille materials, as well as the cost of this production.

There are at least two factors which may impede the widespread application of paperless braillers for some time to come. High initial costs will allow few readers to own them without third party financing. Additionally, the tapes cannot yet be reproduced easily or inexpensively on equipment designed for reproducing audiotapes.

Braille Production

A number of computer terminals are now able to print braille outputs and provide braille versions of the input as well. Some print at speeds up to 120 characters per second and require no programs of other intervention in terms of normal computer operation. One system in France prints braille on both sides of the paper allowing a 50% saving on expensive paper.

A system produced by T.V. Cranmer, Director of the Division of Technical Services, Bureau for the Blind, Frankfort, Kentucky, is designed to be operated by sighted typists who do not know braille. Using a standard keyboard, this person types text into a computer and edits the text on the computer's visual display. The material is then printed out in braille that is close to Grade 2. All of the Grade 2 symbols are utilized, although rules relating to context are not.

Maryland Computer Services (MCS) has a Braille Translation System, similar to Cranmer's system, which is operated by a sighted operator who need not know braille. The user can edit and re-write text after entering it, since the MCS system is based on a word processor.

The advantages offered by computerized braille are obvious. While computerization may ultimately lead to cost reduction in saving paper and storage space, the initial expense is high. Another factor to consider is the difficulty and expense that may be involved in making managerial and personnel practice changes (Mellor, 1979).

Alternatives to Braille

Although there is no medium that can replace braille, a number of sophisticated print-to-touch machines are now available and are being used as supplements to braille.

Reading by listening is an obvious way to gain access to print, and this method can be more efficient (in terms of the interaction between speed and comprehension) than braille. For example, Nolan (1966) found that information taken in by listening required approximately one-third of the time necessary for tactual reading and, furthermore, comprehension remained stable. Compressed speech devices have permitted listening at a rate of 275 words per minute without loss of comprehension (Orr, Friedman, & Williams, 1965). Braille reading is much slower, and reading rates for high school students have been reported at 110 words per minute (Lowenfeld, Abel, & Hatlen, 1969).

Attempts to develop machines than can optically scan printed material and produce intelligible sounds date back to 1919, when the optophone was demonstrated in England. The machine scanned a printed page and produced coded sounds corresponding to printed letters (Jameson, 1966). Few people ever learned to use the machine because it proved difficult to learn the sound code, and reading speeds were slow (Hanninen, 1975).

The Kurzweil Reading Machine (KRM) is one of the most recent print-to-sound devices. It has an automatic tracking device or an optional hand-held scanner that scans print and sends electronic signals to microprocessors, in which rules of grammar and their exceptions have been stored. The microprocessors translate the signals into synthetic speech at 150 words per minute. As with all complex devices, training is required in learning to operate it. Several KRMs are now undergoing evaluation in the field. The cost is still high, some $19,500 for the Desk Top model, though this is less than one-half the price of the first models.

Print-to-touch machines have also been tested. The most widely used is the Optacon (OPtical to TActile CONverter) manufacturerd by Telesensory Systems, Incorporated (TSI). The Optacon allows a blind person to read ordinary print by sensing the letters tactually on a matrix of vibrating pins. A small hand-held scanning device is moved along the lines of print while one finger of the other hand rests on the vibrating pins and detects the shapes of print letters. Weihl (1971) reported Optacon reading rates of 6 to 8 words per minute after 20 hours of instruction for elementary and junior high students. Higher reading rates have been reported for adults using the Optacon regularly and intensively. The highest rate reported has been approximately 80 words per minute (Mangold, 1976). Cost of the machine at the time of this writing is some $3000. TSI is presently working on a speech output device for the Optacon, similar in its capabilities to the previously discussed Kurzweil Reading Machine.

In summary, compressed speech devices provide a means of reading through listening far superior to braille in terms of efficiency. On the other hand, in comparison with recorded materials, braille is more easily scanned, allows random access to information (e.g., for reference works), and is better-suited for displaying tables and some kinds of diagrams. The Kurzweil Reading Machine and the Optacon promise blind individuals immediate access to print that is not possible by conventional braille production techniques. The present size and cost of the Kurzweil Machine prevent it from being a realistic alternative for individuals, though institutions might benefit by making them available. The slow rate of reading achieved with the Optacon likewise prevents it from replacing braille. One might conclude that, at the present time, there are no adequate alternatives to braille. The Optacon, the Kurzweil Machine, and the compressed speech devices are useful supplements to braille for some kinds of reading materials—for those who can afford them or can obtain third party financing. A major priority in the midst of all this technology should therefore be the development of greater efficiency in one's ability to read braille.

Nature of Tactual Reading

Kusajima (1974) conducted an experimental investigation of the physiology and psychology of visual and tactual reading. The comparisons that he drew between the two modes from his investigation are summarized below.

Pause and Movement. In visual reading, the eye moves in a series of rapid jumps: it alternately pauses briefly and then moves again; in this way, fixation on points along a line of text is combined with jumping eye movements. During long pauses, letters, words, or short sentences are perceived all at once; no recognition occurs during jumping movements. Most reading time is spent in pauses (92-98%). In contrast, during braille reading pauses are rare. When the finger stops moving, only the letter under the finger is read. Thus, it may be said that the fingers read braille through movement.

Number and Location of Pauses. When visual reading skills improve, the number of pauses declines and becomes more rhythmic. In braille reading, fewer up-and-down, zig-zag movements and irregular finger pressures indicate increasing skill. For both modes of reading, any means of reducing wasted motion is desirable. The location of pauses in visual and in braille reading is not related to meaning, grammar or rhetoric.

Function of Pauses/Movements. In visual reading, letters, words or short sentences are perceived all at once during pauses, but in braille reading, characters are perceived successively. Thus, the unit of perception is much wider in visual reading than it is in tactual reading. Nevertheless, on the basis of the number of perceptual units covered in braille, it is not as slow as one would predict. This is best explained by regarding the reading process as perception combined with other factors.

Methods of Perception. The best visual readers apprehend sentences through groups of words or even short sentences. For braille readers, Kusajima concludes that letters are perceived successively through movement of the fingers. The best braille readers, then, group letters in perception. It should be noted that Nolan and Kederis (1969) found the basic perceptual unit in braille reading to be the individual braille cell. The fact that most teachers successfully use a whole word method in teaching braille suggests that further research is needed in this area. Crandell (1974) has suggested that two kinds of perceptual windows are employed by a braille reader—one spatial (the braille cell) and the other temporal. Even though each spatial unit must be recognized sequentially, he proposes that a relatively large number of these units are processed in a given time period. Information received through the senses is then accumulated and sequenced into temporal units and processed as a single unit. The more spatial units accommodated in the temporal units, the more total information available to the perceiver. The length of the temporal unit may vary from less than a second to several seconds.

Dominant and Subordinate Characters. In visual reading, word recognition depends on context and shape characteristics; letter shapes may be dominant or subordinate in characterizing the form of a word. The situation is similar in braille reading. The average braille reader obtains clues from the first one, two or three characters in a word; these become the dominant letters in the sentence.

Good and Poor Reading. Good or poor reading is determined by a combination of the reader's ability and experiences, his mechanical habits, as well as the difficulty of the material being read. Good visual reading is characterized by a small number of short regular pauses, no regressive movements, well-adjusted return sweeps, and accurate understanding of the text. Good braille reading is characterized by few zig-zag, up-and-down or fluttering movements, uniform pressure on the fingertips, no regressive movements, coordinated movements between lines with both hands, and accurate textual understanding.

Return Sweeps and Movements Between Lines. Visual return sweeps are generally shorter than the line of text, since the pauses at the beginning and end of the sentence are usually within the line. In one-handed braille reading, return sweep length between successive lines of text are longer than the text line, since tactual verification of the line's beginning and end is necessary. For both types of reading, the eye or finger movements become habituated motor acts. In bi-manual (two-handed) braille reading, the trailing finger helps control the movement of the leading (or reading) finger, preventing over- or under-estimated return sweep movements. While the reading finger finishes one line of text, the trailing finger returns to the location of the beginning of the next line and awaits contact with the reading finger. The reading finger moves quickly to make this contact and then both read along to about the middle of the line. At this point the trailing finger separates to make the return sweep.

Both Eyes and Both Hands. Since the mechanical movement of the eyes in the same direction is involuntary, independent movement of the eyes across different lines of print is physiologically impossible. In contrast, both hands are under voluntary control during braille reading. The accompaniment of the trailing finger widens the perceptual aperture. Reassurance is attained by reading with both hands. A bi-manual reader can "hold" at the place where a point is missed and the reading finger returned to that spot for review. Misprints, spoiled embossed dots, obscure characters, and difficult or unfamiliar words can be indexed by the trailing finger, while the reading finger scans to help organize meaning. It is also possible that fingers on both hands are used for reading, with fingers on either hand serving as the indexers and those of the other hand searchers of meaning through context.

Studies on Braille Reading Habits of Children

There have been several studies of braille reading habits, and the three most comprehensive will be summarized here.

Maxfield (1928) found that two-handed braille readers were superior readers. In addition, right-handed braille readers were more efficient readers than were left-handed readers. She observed that the best readers read ahead with the left hand before finishing the preceding line with the right hand. Further suggestions made by Maxfield as a result of her study were: 1) The fingertips should not be pressed down too heavily: 2) Children should be taught to read with both hands; 3) Excessive up-and-down motion of the finger tips should be discouraged; 4) Books should be held parallel with the edge of the table or at a narrow, acute angle; and 5) Lip movement and inner speech should be discouraged since they retard reading speed.

Bürklen (1932) tested 66 readers and found that one-fourth of them had no hand preference for reading braille; three-fourths of this group read slightly better with the left hand than with the right hand—which is inconsistent with Maxfield's findings. Bürklen further found that the index fingers of both hands were best for reading, with the middle fingers used secondarily, and other fingers still less frequently. Touch movements of good readers proceeded in a straight line, while those of poor readers were serrated and twisted. As in Maxfield's study, pressure of the fingertips was more slight and uniform among good readers than among poor readers. He observed that touch sensitivity decreased only a small amount after several hours of braille reading. General fatigue was also found to be negligible after extended braille reading. Bürklen's subjects read, on the average, three to four times slower than sighted print individuals. One must remember, however, that he used Grade 1—uncontracted—braille in his study. Reading with both hands was found to be the most efficient among his subjects; single-handed braille readers nearly doubled their reading times. Bürklen concluded that arm and body positions were important to efficient braille reading as well. Along these lines, he suggested that book height be such that arm and hand movements were unhampered. He recognized that in braille the most-used letters were not identical with the most readable ones.

Several changes occurred in the teaching of braille reading after the Maxfield and Bürklen studies. Grade 2 (contracted) braille began to be introduced from the beginning of reading instruction. Braille printing underwent changes, which made braille books more available and less expensive. Methods of teaching braille also changed.

Lowenfeld, Abel and Hatlen (1969) conducted a study in an attempt to assess the effects of some of these changes. Two hundred blind students attending public or residential schools were participants. Half the students were fourth-graders and half were eighth-graders. An analysis of the reading behavior of these students showed:

(1) There was no significant difference in reading comprehension and rate scores among students using the left hand, the right hand, or both hands; (2) Eighth graders who found the next line with their left hand and read ahead with it while the right hand finished the preceding line, were more efficient readers than their peers who did not use this method; (3) Superior

braille readers tended to read in an even flow, not to rub letters, not to lose their places in reading, and not to accompany their reading with silent speech movements; (4) Students who read without mannerisms and were more relaxed while reading were superior readers; (5) Posture during reading appeared to have no influence on reading efficiency; and (6) "Avid" braille readers were superior readers.

Attempts to Increase the Efficiency of Braille Reading

Studies by Umsted (1972) and Wallace (1973) have demonstrated that training in rapid recognition of the braille cell significantly increases braille reading rates. Wallace found further that a group receiving rapid reading training alone exceeded the rate gain made by a group receiving such training coupled with recognition training. His conclusion was that recognition training may have interfered with the rapid reading training in that two distinct and opposing perceptual units were involved in the two treatments. Recognition training stressed code accuracy, while the key factor in rapid reading training was speed. The perceptual unit in recognition training was presumably spatial and was initially the braille cell. On the other hand, the perceptual unit during rapid reading was predominantly temporal in nature.

Grunwald (1966) studied the possible efficiency of braille reading through the use of a device that continuously moved sheets of paper (embossed with braille characters) over a platen at precisely controlled rates or in accurately timed steps. A maximum sweep rate of 320 words per minute was achieved with this device on different types of reading material. He observed that braille readers did not slow down when they became unsure of the meaning of what they were reading; instead, they seemed to read intermittently. A major conclusion of his study was that braille readers perceived patterns in time rather than in space; they are concerned with rhythm rather than geometry. He further stated that the braille reading process is not static; it is accomplished through movement, and therefore differs from print reading. The maximum sweep rate found in the study could not have provided readers time to resolve inter-character dot distance or the distance between dots of the same cell. Thus, readers were not grasping the "real geometry" of each braille character. Grunwald advocated the use of mechanical devices, similar to those in his study, for helping beginning readers make the transition from studying static braille cell geometry to dynamic reading of braille.

Various mechanical devices (i.e., tachistoscopes) have been used experimentally to increase braille reading rates; typically these devices move braille or type from right to left across an exposed presentation window. Heber (1967) found three of these devices were successful in improving the braille reading rates of children (grades three to nine) and adults when compared with control groups. On the other hand, Kederis (1971) found no significant increase in braille reading rates using two such machines. Both experimental and control groups achieved similar gains in braille reading rate when given monetary rewards for improvement.

McBride (1974) reported on one of several workshops he had conducted for teaching visually handicapped adults to read braille more rapidly. Using rapid reading techniques similar to those for teaching print readers, McBride reported a group rate increase from 138 words per minute to 710 words per minute after two weeks of training. One participant reportedly increased her rate from 144 words per minute to 1600 words per minute. Comprehension was not measured by a formal test, but rather by informal estimates on prose fiction after oral questioning. The level of comprehension admittedly dropped somewhat according to McBride.

Olson (1975) reported having tested 15 adult participants in an August 1974 rapid braille reading workshop taught by McBride. Significant rate gains were achieved by this group on both a formal test and an informal test (similar to those McBride employed) without significant loss in comprehension. The rate increase on the formal test was, however, considerably more modest (30 + %) when compared to the rate increase on the informal test (200 + %). Olson further taught a similar workshop for large print and braille readers using McBride's rapid reading techniques. Her braille group was similar in size, age, sex, and ability level to McBride's group. Instead of the participants seeking to enroll in the workshop (as was true for McBride's group), Olson's subjects were recruited and were simultaneously engaged in jobs or school. Even though Olson's group had significantly fewer years of education and practiced five times less than McBride's group, rate and comprehension results were strikingly comparable after two weeks of rapid reading training. A rate gain of 45% was achieved on the formal test, while a 220% increase in rate was found on the informal test. As with McBride's group, comprehension did not change significantly. Olson concluded that the large discrepancy between the informal and formal tests may have indicated: (1) Participants' inability to effectively employ rapid reading techniques on the formal test because of the propensity to search for possible "test questions"; and/or (2) Participants overestimating their levels of comprehension on the informal tests. Additional findings by Olson included: (1) Rates predicted by braille readers before the start of rapid reading training did not significantly differ from rates achieved on informal tests after training; (2) Rate improvements made by braille readers were not significantly related to their pre-training rates; (3) Rate improvement after rapid reading training was negatively related to the age of participants and the number of years braille readers had previously read print; and (4) Rate improvement after rapid reading training was positively related to the use of more than one finger in the braille reading process.

Recommendations from her study emphasized the need for incorporating reading techniques into the beginning instructional program for braille readers, the value of multiple finger use and independent hand movement in braille reading, as well as the necessity of further research on rapid braille reading. The effects of motivation, amount compared with type of practice employed, and the retention of rate gains, were pointed out as some areas requiring further investigation.

Common Instructional Approaches to Braille

A survey on the status of braille reading instruction was reported by Lowenfeld, Abel and Hatlen (1969) as a result of questionnaires sent to 289 teachers of blind children in local schools and 73 teachers in residential schools. They found that most local and residential schools for the blind began braille reading instruction in the first grade, after some pre-reading instruction in kindergarten. Approximately one-third of the schools started reading instruction by teaching the braille alphabet, while two-thirds began with whole words and/or meaningful sentences. Nearly all schools used Grade 2 braille from the beginning. Approximately 85% of the teachers encouraged the use of both hands; the remaining teachers encouraged use of the right hand. Two-thirds of the teachers encouraged the use of both index fingers; varying finger combinations were emphasized by the rest of the teachers. The braille writer was used almost universally to teach beginning writing. Half of the teachers in both types of schools introduced it at the same time as reading, and about one-third reported that they did so after some reading skill had developed. Local schools reported that initial braille instruction was given by resource teachers (51%), itinerant teachers (29%), classroom teachers (9%), and by special braille teachers (9%). In residential schools, classroom teachers (90%) and special braille teachers (10%) provided this instruction.

A smaller sample of teachers (20 residential, 41 local) from the above-mentioned study provided further specific information about the beginning braille instruction. Local schools introduced books (including pre-primers) at the beginning of braille reading instruction, or after words or sentences were read. Most residential schools, on the other hand, introduced reading books only after words or sentences were read. Both oral and silent reading instruction were reported, and double-spaced material was universally used in beginning instruction. The use of enlarged braille had nearly disappeared at the time of this survey.

Among the current methodologies described for teaching reading are the basal reader approach, the phonetic approach, the linguistic approach, the language experience approach, and the modified alphabet approach. Research on these methods of teaching reading to children has not established the superiority of any one method (Lowenfeld, 1973). Lowenfeld pointed out that teachers must be cognizant of all approaches so that appropriate systems can be adapted or combined to accommodate individual children. The American Printing House for the Blind is now field testing reading materials which recognize the difference between braille and print reading. A set of specifications for the series was compiled after research into braille reading, tactual perception, concept development (of blind children) and current teaching practices was completed. These specifications were used to select vocabulary, teaching methodology and areas of special emphasis (Caton, 1979).

References

Bürklen, K. *Touch reading of the blind.* New York: American Foundation for the Blind, 1932.

Caton, H. A primary reading program for beginning braille readers. *Journal of Visual Impairment and Blindness,* 1979, **73**(8), 309-313.

Crandell, J. Rapid reading in braille: Fact or fancy. *dvh Newsletter,* 1974, **19**, 3-5.

Grunwald, A. On reading and reading braille. Bethesda, Maryland: ERIC Document Reproduction Service, ED 104831, 1966.

Hanninen, K. *Teaching the visually handicapped.* Columbus, OH: Charles Merrill Publishing Company, 1975.

Heber, R. A study of programmed instruction in braille. Bethesda, MD: ERIC Document Reproduction Service, ED 015303, 1967.

Jameson, J. The octophone: Its beginning and development. *Bulletin of Prosthetic Research.* Washington, D.C.: Veteran's Administration, 1966, 25-28.

Kederis, C. Training for increasing braille reading rates. Bethesda, MD: ERIC Document Reproduction Service, ED 023229, 1971.

Kusajima, T. *Visual reading and braille reading: An experimental investigation of the physiology and psychology of visual and tactual reading.* New York: American Foundation for the Blind, 1974.

Lowenfeld, B., Abel, G., & Hatlen, P. *Blind children learn to read.* Springfield, IL: Charles C Thomas, 1969.

Lowenfeld, B. *The visually handicapped child in school.* New York: John Day Company, 1973.

Mangold, S. *The effects of a developmental teaching approach on tactile perception and braille letter recognition based on a precision teaching model.* San Francisco: California State University, San Francisco, 1976.

Maxfield, K. *The blind child and his reading.* New York: American Foundation for the Blind, 1932.

McBride, V. Exploration of rapid reading in braille. *New Outlook for the Blind,* 1974, **68**, 8-13.

Mellor, C.M. Technical Innovations for braille reading, writing, and production. *Journal of Visual Impairment and Blindness,* 1979, **73**(8), 339-341.

Nolan, C. *Reading and listening in learning by the blind: Progress Report.* Louisville, KY: American Printing House for the Blind, 1966.

Nolan, C. Thoughts on the future of braille. *Journal of Visual Impairment and Blindness,* 1979, **73**(8), 333-335.

Nolan, C., & Kederis, C. *Perceptual factors in braille word recognition.* New York: American Foundation for the Blind, 1969.

Olson, M. *The effects of training in rapid reading on the reading rate and comprehension of braille and large print readers.* Ann Arbor, MI: University Microfilms International, 1975.

Orr, D., Friedman, H., & Williams, J. Trainability of listening comprehension of speeded discourse. *Journal of Educational Psychology*, 1965, **56**, 148-156.

Umsted, R. *Improvement of braille reading through code recognition and training.* Ann Arbor, MI: University Microfilms International, 1970.

Wallace, D. The effect of rapid reading instruction and recognition training on the reading rate and comprehension of adult legally blind print and braille readers. Unpublished doctoral dissertation, Brigham Young University, 1973.

Weihl, C. The Optacon reading program at the Monroe Public School. *New Outlook for the Blind,* 1971, **65**, 155-162.

Chapter III
Pre-School Experiences
Important to Braille
Reading Readiness

In assessing any child's readiness to read, the teacher must consider such factors as mental age, physical maturation, social-emotional development, experiential background, oral language skills, sensory acuity, sensory efficiency, and motivation. Lowenfeld (1973) points out that visually handicapped children need a period of reading readiness beyond that required for sighted children.

It is the purpose of this chapter to discuss four areas related to reading readiness that are of particular importance in teaching blind children. Specific suggestions are given to parent and pre-school teachers of blind children for the development of: (1) Early sensory-motor abilities; (2) Sensory acuity and efficiency; (3) Basic concepts; and (4) Reading awareness.

Sensory-motor Development

We generally think of the first 24 months of life as the sensory-motor period. A longitudinal study of blind infants has found that deprivation of experiences during this period can result in severe ego disturbances (Fraiberg, 1968). Furthermore, the infants' lack of sight clearly demanded specific adaptations of the sensory experiences normally provided for sighted babies.

Human Attachment. The learning process begins with a child's interaction with his environment. Human attachment is typically the first step of this interaction. While sighted infants have the advantage of visually tracking or focusing upon their parents, blind infants must find a tactile-auditory language that will bring them into this first human partnership. Fraiberg (1968) noted that many parents felt at a loss as to how they could establish bonds of attachment with their blind newborn babies. Pre-school workers have found empty baby books and feelings of hopelessness among these parents as a group.

It is essential that parents talk to their blind infants and verbalize their interactions with them during bathing, feeding, diapering, and dressing. Blind babies also require a great deal of cuddling. Because premature blind infants often resist being cuddled, parents may have to be extremely persistent in their efforts (Fraiberg, 1968).

Parents should expect the motor development of their blind infants to progress at a slower pace than for sighted infants. While a sighted child usually learns to lift his head from prone by age one month, the blind child lacks the visual stimulation to do this. One might tickle the blind infant's chin or kiss his forehead in an attempt to tactually stimulate this movement. Although it is important to expose the blind infant to sound, it must be understood that he will be unable to localize it until he is about nine months old. Subsequent skills of sitting, standing, and walking alone may also occur later for blind children. This delay exists not only because there is no visual stimulation to motivate these activities, but also because the development of balance is more difficult to achieve without the visual sense.

Discovery of Objects. As previously mentioned, blind infants cannot use sound as an adaptive substitute for vision until they are some nine months old. Blind babies tend to care only about their bottles and pacifiers if not deliberately introduced to toys. Toys needs to be presented in a limited space and should be tactually interesting. Cradle gyms or mobiles that make noise are good. Rattles should be placed directly into the blind child's hands. Helping him to shake the rattle in order to produce sound will help to develop the sense of "causality."

As soon as blind infants sit unsupported, a broad surfaced, three-sided play table may be helpful for placing favorite toys in front of them for tactual exploration. A playpen equipped with bells, wind-up toys, or portable radios is especially appropriate for children eight to twelve months of age. Generally speaking, toys that are pushed give blind infants a better sense of their bodies with respect to objects than do pull-toys. Household items, nesting toys, rhythm instruments, records, and music boxes are additional favorites among blind children.

Children without vision need assistance and longer periods of time to compare the sizes and shapes of objects in their environment. Whenever possible, parents should permit free exploration of at least one cupboard or drawer to enhance such generalizations. Sighted children quickly determine the use of objects through visual observation. Parents and pre-school teachers of the blind must deliberately "show" object function and further help the children distinguish among "real" objects and "models" or representations.

Prehension (grasping). For the first six months of the blind infant's life his hands usually remain fisted, showing little play at midline. Sighted infants reach and grasp objects for midline examination by the time they are five months old, but this level of coordination skill does not usually occur before ten or eleven months among blind infants (Fraiberg, 1977). Parents will need to physically guide their infants' hands to the bottle during feeding. Toys introduced at the midline (with some physical guidance of the child's hands to explore them) will also be important. Patty-cake and similar lap games provide verbal stimulation to accompany midline play.

Locomotion. It has already been pointed out that motor development is directly tied to incentive for movement. Fraiberg (1968) found that the babies in her study did not walk earlier than 17 months of age. There is also a certain amount of anxiety that results from launching into the unknown. Parents, too, will naturally worry about their blind child's safety. It will be important to guard against the resulting temptation to "overprotect." A reasonably safe play space should be fenced off for the blind child's independent exploration. Sharp objects or heavy objects that are easily tipped may be removed, but minor falls and bumps should not be prevented.

Since motor movements may not be initiated by blind babies, parents and pre-school teachers will have to manipulate them into movements from birth. Rockers and bouncing chairs help these infants safely release pent-up tension and energy.

Sensory Acuity and Efficiency

When the visual sense is functioning with a high degree of efficiency, children make fundamental use of this sense for understanding and expanding their environment. Data provided by all the other senses usually become supplementary. Visually handicapped children, on the other hand, may need to rely more heavily on other senses, while developing the visual sense as supplementary. Although the tactual-kinesthetic and auditory channels are the two most vital to the braille reader, the development of acuity and efficiency in all sensory channels will be discussed. The rationale for this is that a blind child relates to the braille symbols on a page to the extent he can extract the meaning that they represent. Furthermore, meaning is expanded with growth in the braille reader's experiences and his ability to integrate experiences achieved through all sensory channels.

Tactual-kinesthetic Sense. Révész (1950) suggests that clear impressions cannot be gained tactually unless touching involves movement. Because the tactual and kinesthetic senses are so highly interrelated, they will be discussed simultaneously.

Lowenfeld (1973) maintains that babies have two main sources of stimulation for the "skin senses" during their first few weeks of life—the reflexive movements of their own bodies and the touch and tender handling of those caring for them. In the blind infant, manipulation of the limbs causes the kinesthetic receptors to provide information about body space and awareness of the possibilities of movement within that space (Cratty, 1971). It is believed that such manipulation is received passively at the unconscious perceptual level, but storage of motor patterns may contribute to later cognitive development.

Because blind infants cannot visually guide their hands to explore the environment, planned stimulation must be provided. The adults in the children's environments must therefore give physical guidance during explorations and verbally describe differences among things they touch.

Before they start to explore with their hands, infants gain a wide variety of information through their mouths. Thus, it is essential that blind children have opportunities to suck and mouth foods of different consistencies as well as objects which are pleasing and safe.

Initial stimulation of the hands is best encouraged through textures that are soft and warm to the touch. Until babies develop voluntary grasp reactions and begin exploring with purpose, one should provide soft objects with little variation in contour—the emphasis, then, being only upon texture (Lowenfeld, 1973). Parents and pre-school teachers should experiment with the tactual preferences of blind infants and gradually introduce new textures to arouse their interests.

Relationships have been found to exist among tactual ability, mental age, and measured intelligence; since chronological age has been found to be unrelated to tactual ability, the ability to discriminate tactually is apparently developmental in nature as well as a learned skill (Hammill and Crandell, 1968). The following tactual activities, arranged developmentally, might be used with blind pre-schoolers. They represent a compilation of ideas from a variety of sources (Lowenfeld, 1973; Hanninen, 1975; Harrell, 1977).

Ages 6-12 months

1) Present toys that are tactually pleasant and not too small to examine or grasp.
2) Encourage play with nesting toys such as cardboard boxes, barrels, cups, and toy blocks; start with large items and work toward the smaller ones.
3) Introduce toys that are highly manipulative: busy boxes, work benches, wind-up toys, music boxes.
4) In guiding tactual exploration, give the child word names and action verbs to accompany his actions.

Ages 1-2½ years

1) Provide finger foods and hard-to-tip drinking cups; allow self-feeding.
2) Verbally describe the tactual qualities of objects in the child's environment (soft pillow, cold milk, hot stove, hard floor).
3) Provide household items that demand finer motor manipulations: lids and pans, keys and locks, large nuts and bolts.
4) Help the child manipulate his own body, then the body of a doll or another person while you speak the name of the body part and describe the movement.

Ages 2½-3½ years

1) Give the child size references: use articles of clothing that belong to family members, his toys or dishes.

2) Have the child sort family shoes into pairs. Use other objects for sorting according to similarities of size, length, shape: blocks, beads, buttons, silverware.

3) Encourage the child to manipulate clothing fasteners such as buttons, hooks, and zippers.

4) Play copy-cat games for bead-stringing and block building.

5) Glue materials to a deck of playing cards and have the child match pairs according to texture; make initial pairs grossly different (sandpaper, wool, plastic, flannel).

6) Give the child a number of containers to open; have him practice opening doors.

7) Give the child play-doh, clay, slime or finger paints to manipulate.

Ages 4-5 years

1) Introduce beads smaller than those previously used, and have the child string them.

2) Have the child help set the table and dust furniture.

3) Encourage independent dressing, except for small hooks and ties.

4) Have the child brush his teeth unassisted.

5) Encourage bathing with minimal assistance.

6) Introduce cutting and pasting; have the child make a "touch scrapbook" of interesting textures and shapes.

7) When taking a walk, have the child identify differences among walking surfaces (sidewalk, dirt, grass, pavement).

8) Encourage the child to make replicas of real objects with clay; illustrate body movements with the use of clay.

9) Introduce three dimensional geometric figures; make raised line drawings of them for the child to explore. Finally have the child make a raised line interpretation of a shape.

10) When teaching concepts (discussed later) use tactual concept books with two dimensional figures.

The general *Catalog of Tangible Apparatus*, available from the American Printing House for the Blind, lists a number of items that may be useful in teaching tactual discrimination. Some of these are listed below:

1) Aluminum diagramming sheets for drawing diagrams.

2) Constructo sets that include large pieces of hardwood with wooden bolts.

3) Plastic or wooden pegboads and pegs.

4) Squares of cardboard perforated for sewing.

5) *Roughness Discrimination Test* used to predict braille reading readiness.

6) Form board with removable hand imprints.

7) *Touch and Tell* series (reading readiness book designed for blind children).

8) Shoelace aid to teach lacing and tying.
9) Giant textured beads to illustrate solids of varying size, shape, and texture.
10) Shape board consisting of a tray with pegs on which five different shapes (in three sizes) are hung as a sorting task.
11) Swail dot inverter for hand embossing of lines.

Auditory Sense. Stimulation of the auditory sense is important for blind children even before they are able to use their tactual-kinesthetic senses. The soothing sound of voices paired with physical cuddling is the first means of establishing and maintaining contact with their environment (Lowenfeld, 1973). The first functional level of sound is that of primitive environmental noises; the signal and warning level comes next, after which the symbolic level for reception of speech sounds becomes functional (Frisina, 1967).

Of great importance for the development of auditory discrimination skills is the factor of attention. If the auditory stimulation provided does not give meaningful information, the child remains at a mechanical level of sound reception. Too often blind children are left alone to be stimulated by noise (radio, television) and consequently learn rote repetitions of words, phrases, and jingles. The visually handicapped child needs frequent vocal stimulation and interaction, first with adults and then with other children. A tactual-auditory dialogue forms a basis for his learning and helps him establish a perceptual frame of reference. Clarification of auditory perceptions comes through others listening to his responses and by answering his questions about himself and the environment. Allowing a child to engage in meaningless auditory self-stimulation without interjecting thought-provoking conversations makes no contribution to his perceptual development (Lowenfeld, 1973).

Auditory discrimination ability appears to increase with the child's development up to age seven or eight (Hammill & Crandell, 1969). Foulke (1968) suggests that listening skills can and should be taught to blind children in order to increase their intake of information that is either unavailable in braille or too slowly read tactually. It should be noted that reading aurally is a very different perceptual task from reading visually: The acoustical display to be coded and processed is controlled by the rate of input of the reading medium rather than by the reader himself (Foulke, 1967). Because the only information available to an aural reader is in one time dimension, a sound cannot be recalled for consideration once it has passed. Unless the words are remembered, processed, and coded as heard, the reader's perception may be inaccurate, distorted, or completely meaningless. Even though aural reading offers many advantages to blind children, far more attention ought be given to maximizing listening ability for the most efficient organization of word sequences into chunks of information that can be associated with previous and subsequent learning (Miller, 1967).

Below is a list of developmental activities that might be carried out by parents and teachers wishing to enhance auditory acuity and efficiency of visually handicapped pre-schoolers (Lowenfeld, 1973; Hanninen, 1975; Harrell, 1977):

0-6 months
1) Family members should speak to the baby whenever entering his room.
2) Limit the exposure to "artificial sounds" of television and radio.

6-12 months
1) Present sound toys, changing their positions. Encourage the child's pursuit through reaching or head turning.
2) Play relaxing music at the child's nap time.
3) Call to the child from various directions and immediately follow with a gentle stroke from the same direction on a corresponding body part.

1-2½ years
1) Continue introducing new sound toys (radios, rhythm records, balls with bells inside).
2) Play hide and seek.
3) Have the child touch noise-making household items and point out sounds they make: toilet, faucet, drawers, crinkling paper, vacuum, refrigerator, clock, furnace.
4) Take neighborhood walks pointing out sounds: cars, dogs, toys, wind, trees.
5) Take the child to a local supermarket and point out sounds: watering of vegetables, carts bumping, cash register ringing.

2½-4 years
1) Introduce more advanced sound toys (coins in a bank, rhythm instruments).
2) During walks outdoors, ask the child what he hears.
3) Take field trips to a variety of stores, zoos, farms, and other places to hear new sounds.
4) Play word games with the child using animal sounds.
5) Encourage the child to imitate sounds he hears.
6) Do body movements to records.
7) Tape record familiar sounds and ask him to identify them.
8) Hide a music box that is playing and have the child find it.

4-5 years
1) Have the child run simple errands that require short-term memory.

2) Play games involving guessing how the speaker is "feeling" according to his tone of voice.
3) Have the child identify television programs by their theme songs, voices, background sounds.
4) Point out how sounds differ when listened to from inside vs. outside; expose him to constant vs. intermittent sound.
5) Have the child respond with body movements to sounds that are loud vs. soft in tone, high vs. low in pitch, fast vs. slow in tempo.
6) Play a tape of sounds and ask the child to make up a story around the sounds.
7) Demonstrate the sounds of ten objects on a tray and name them for the child; ask the child to name them from the sound they produce.
8) Make up poems and stories with obvious ending words missing; ask the child to offer a rhyming word from your example.
9) Have the child clap whenever he hears a rhyming word. Example: Words that rhyme with "bat" in the book *The Cat in the Hat* by Dr. Seuss.
10) Play the game "Gossip," in which a message is passed through whispering successively down a line of people.
11) Discuss the importance of sound for safety purposes.

Visual Sense. If visually impaired children have even a small amount of vision, efforts should be made to help them use it efficiently. In addition to the sequential development of visual abilities, a number of environmental conditions and psychological characteristics appear to have a direct influence on the development and use of visual capacities. Lighting conditions appropriate for some children are not suitable for others. Likewise, there are individual differences with respect to the amount of contrast needed to distinguish figure and ground of materials. Attitude, personality, mental capacity, physical stamina, and motivation are thought to have a close relationship to visual performance (Lowenfeld, 1973). Groups of low vision children who have participated in experimental programs of visual stimulation have shown gains in visual performance (Barraga, 1964).

A brief list of activities for enhancing the visual efficiency of children is given below (Barraga, 1970; Lowenfeld, 1973; Harrell, 1977):

6-12 months
1) Place mobiles over the child's crib; physically guide his hands to them and face his head in the right direction.
2) Provide brightly colored toys to attract the child's attention; initially provide a sound clue to help the child locate the toy.
3) Project lighting over the child's shoulder rather than directly into his face.

1-2½ years
1) Encourage the child to explore toys visually; do not try to alter the way he holds objects for examination, because it may thwart further examination.
2) Call the child's attention to colors of clothes, walls, food, and all other familiar objects in his surroundings. Provide identifying terminology to encourage association with visual sensations.

2½-4 years
1) Make it a habit for the child to search for toys, replacing them in a box when he is finished playing with them.
2) Encourage play with crayons and paper; try attaching paper to flannel board covered with screen for children with minimal vision. The crayons should leave a tactual line as a result of the rough screen surface.
3) Help the child to build block towers and string beads by color.
4) Help the child make visual size comparisons with nesting toys, clothing, furniture, trees and plants, vehicles, etc.

4-5 years
1) Show the child pictures of real objects; as a game, have him match them with real objects.
2) Have the child sort objects by shape, size, and color (spoons, shoes, blocks, toys).
3) Expose the child to large picture books, having him point out familiar objects, colors, etc.

Olfactory Sense. Pleasant odors are often a means of leading visually handicapped children toward objects or events to which they cannot be drawn by vision (Lowenfeld, 1973). As they grow older, perception of certain odors will become a source of spatial orientation needed for independent travel. It is for these reasons that attention should be given to developing the sense of smell in visually handicapped children. Parents and teachers need to point out smells in the house, school, or neighborhood that will serve to supplement their knowledge of the environment. Games can be made of identifying foods or other substances placed in "smell jars." Safety factors that are tied to smell should be discussed as soon as children are old enough to understand, e.g., the smell of gas, burning.

Gustatory Sense. Because of their close physical proximity, the sense organs of smell and taste work in unison much of the time. As an individual tastes an object or food, he also smells it. This phenomenon provides guidance and safety to a visually handicapped infant. Pleasant odors are not always equally appealing to the taste, nor are unpleasant smells always indicative of displeasing taste. Nevertheless, the use of these two senses does provide valuable information to be processed and used with other sensory data (Lowenfeld, 1973). Blind children should be introduced to a variety of foods, even if there is resistance at first. They will need help in testing the temperature of foods before eating in order to avoid the unpleasant associations mouth burns would produce. When children are old enough to open doors, they should be encouraged to get their own simple snacks from the refrigerator or cupboard. By including blind children in mealtime conversation, they can learn the important skill of socializing while eating.

Concept Development

Basic concept formation is what underlies every area of the curriculum. Unlike sighted children, who attain good concept development through visual assimilation, visually handicapped children must have concepts specifically taught to them (Lydon & McGraw, 1973). In order to teach concepts to blind children it is important to first understand concept development among sighted children and then to determine how the process is altered by the lack of vision.

Sighted children appear to develop concepts in the following manner (Lydon & McGraw, 1973):

1) Objects are recognized as existing, differing from one another, and having permanence.
2) Objects are identified and named.
3) Specific characteristics of objects are defined.
4) Common elements of objects are abstracted from sensory experiences and used as defining characteristics of a class.
5) A concept is formed when generalizations about the class are achieved by a symbol.

In moving through the steps outlined above, sighted children progress through three levels of attainment (Zweibelson & Barg, 1967). The first level is described as *concrete*, at which point children consider a specific characteristic of an object to be its content. The second level is *functional*. At this point the content of an object is identified as what it does or what one does with it. The highest level of attainment is reached when children are able to summarize all of the major characteristics of an object; this is described as the *abstract* level.

Blind children lack the visual sense which serves to ''unify'' and establish the wholeness of objects at a distance. They must learn about objects through tactual manipulation and, in most instances, work from part to whole. Handling an object is generally inadequate for establishing its depth, intricacy, or totality. Furthermore, once the object is removed from the blind child's physical grasp, it is gone. In a similar fashion, sounds that are not attached to meaningful and understood sources will fade into nothingness. Blind children, therefore, take much longer to develop a sense of object permanency (Cutsforth, 1951). Because of the limited effectiveness of the tactual sense, the blind child usually has only partial success in progressing from the concrete and functional levels to the abstract level of concept development (Zweibelson & Barg, 1967).

General Guidelines for Teaching Concepts to Blind Children. Lydon & McGraw (1973) have outlined a number of important guidelines for teaching concepts to children with severe visual impairment. These are summarized below:

1) Adults and children often misunderstand one another because they use the same words but these words may have very different meanings. Check to make certain there is consistency in the terminology used.
2) A child is often more impressed with the concrete externals of a situation than with its essential features. It is difficult for him to distinguish between his own feelings and outside events. These distinctions may have to be deliberately taught.
3) Concepts cannot be taught verbally; they must be founded upon activity.
4) Many children can adequately describe something verbally without having a real understanding of it. Test the concept by having the child show you that he understands.
5) There is need to eliminate "visually oriented" terms in describing things to blind children.
6) Tactual materials that are too complex may be clear to the sighted but confusing to the blind. Blindfold yourself and explore the material tactually to test its effectiveness.
7) It is important to capitalize on the "teachable moment," allowing the child to initiate the learning activity when feasible.
8) An authoritative approach in teaching highly structured beliefs limits questioning on the part of the child. Encourage free exploration.
9) Vocabulary used to teach the child a concept should remain consistent among those having contact with him.

Ways of Teaching Specific Concepts to Pre-Schoolers. Whenever possible, one should use objects closely related to the child in teaching basic concepts—parts of his body, his clothing, his toys, his furniture, his utensils. It will be crucial to develop the blind child's spatial awareness and body image as early as possible, since this will help him interact with his environment in learning all other concepts.

A list of specific concepts and pertinent teaching materials and situations that Harrell (1977) has suggested for teaching visually impaired pre-schoolers is given on pages 30–31:

1) *Likenesses - differences*
   a) matching spoons and forks
   b) clothing
   c) parts of the body
   d) chairs
   e) doors
   f) plants

2) *Small - medium - large*
   a) nesting toys
   b) pots and pans
   c) dishes
   d) clothes
   e) shoes
   f) toys

3) *Big - little*
   a) people
   b) clothing
   c) chairs
   d) toys
   e) quantities of food

4) *Shapes*
   a) Circle: glasses, cups, dishes, doorknobs
   b) Square: windows, some pillows, bottoms of milk cartons
   c) Triangles: tops of milk cartons, roofs on doll houses
   d) Rectangles: doors, some windows, couch cushions, toys

5) *In - out*
   a) boxes
   b) nesting toys
   c) spoons in a pot
   d) climb in a wagon or a car
   e) out of the house
   f) in the yard
   g) foot in the shoe

6) *Up - down*
   a) stairs
   b) reaching exercises
   c) up on the shelf
   d) walk down the stairs

7) *Top - bottom*
   a) clothing
   b) drawers
   c) shelves
   d) doors

8) *Over - under*
   a) over the puddle
   b) under trees
   c) total involvement exercises
   d) toys

9) *On top - underneath*
   a) placing objects places
   b) on top of the blanket
   c) underneath the covers

10) *Wide - narrow*
   a) hallways
   b) sidewalks
   c) sleeve holes and necks of clothing
   d) toys

11) *Sound matching*
   a) different bells
   b) spoons banging pots
   c) cans with noisemaker
   d) toys
   e) musical instruments

12) *Depth*
   a) glasses
   b) steps
   c) cups
   d) water in a tub

13) *Thick - thin*
   a) materials in clothing
   b) carpets
   c) pillows
   d) foods
   e) batters (cake vs. cookie)

14) *Texture matching*
   a) sweaters
   b) coats
   c) drapes
   d) towels
   e) upholstery

15) *Hard - soft*
   a) pillows
   b) floor
   c) rugs
   d) toys

16) *Rough - smooth*
   a) walls
   b) floors
   c) table tops
   d) counters

17) *Front - back*
   a) clothing
   b) houses
   c) lines in school

18) *Number sequences: 1st, 2nd, 3rd*
   a) waiting a turn
   b) races with toys
   c) days of the week, month

19) *Left - right*
   a) arms, legs
   b) clothing
   c) directions

Additional concepts might include: around, away, by, near/far, here/there, off/on, open/close, to/from, front/back, middle/back, first/last, above/below, never/always, once/always, now/then. The *Boehm Test of Basic Concepts*, available from the American Printing House for the Blind, is a good assessment instrument for determining which concepts blind children have mastered before entering school. Each item in the test has been adapted for use with blind children.

Reading Awareness

Sighted children become aware of written words long before they are able to read them. They see adults reading newspapers and books for pleasure and become motivated to learn the skill. Blind children, on the other hand, do not receive the same type of early exposure to braille. When braille is mentioned, it is usually with reference to its being the "last resort." If a child cannot read print, then he will be forced to use braille. Whether or not we actually say braille is "inferior" to print, children seem to pick up that message. Parents and teachers need to make deliberate efforts to expose pre-school blind children to braille in many varied, positive ways.

Modelling Good Braille Reading. Just as sighted children are exposed to print through good reading models, blind children need to have contact with good braille reading models. They should be given the opportunity to tactually observe a braille reader reading for pleasure. After being shown how to move their fingers over the braille symbols, blind children might be encouraged to "follow along" while a sighted person reads the corresponding print in a child's book. Parents will want to discuss reading in front of the child, expressing the value of this skill in their everyday lives.

Labelling Objects with Braille. Braille labels should be attached in strategic locations for the blind child's observation. If he will be facing the object (e.g., a door), the label should be upright at the approximate reach of the child. Labels that might be read by reaching down (e.g., back of a chair) should be affixed upside-down in order to read right-side-up to the child's touch.

Objects selected for labelling should be those most familiar to the blind child. Furthermore, the words used to label these objects should be those the child uses (e.g., the proper name of a favorite toy). Following are some suggestions for objects that might be labelled:

Younger children	*Older children*
1) beds	1) desks
2) chairs	2) refrigerator
3) tables	3) washer/dryer
4) doors	4) stove
5) drawers	5) radio/stereo
6) cupboards	6) bathtub
7) cups	7) food products
8) walls	8) faucets
9) hallways	9) wastebasket
10) stairs	10) dog bowl
11) toothbrush	11) toys
12) clothes	
13) coat hook	

It is a good idea if labels are written in Grade 2 braille, since this is what children will encounter in school. The beginnings of words should be preceded by some kind of symbol to avoid reading labels upside-down. To promote sharing with sighted members of the family, the corresponding print should be provided with each braille label. If clear braille labels are used, the braille label can be placed directly over the print. Where a braille label maker is used, the print can be written above the braille. For labels on braille paper or Brailon, printing can be done on the strip itself.

Each new label made should be introduced to the child by guiding his fingers across the word in the proper direction first. Without forcing the issue, subtly reinforce the concept of starting from the beginning indicator of each word. When the child is ready for details, descriptive word combinations might be introduced on labels (e.g., daddy's chair, front door) (Harrell, 1977).

If there is no resource, itinerant, or residential school teacher to help parents braille labels or children's reading material, the Library of Congress should be contacted for a list of local volunteers.

Providing Memorized Material in Braille. Nursery rhymes, short poems, songs and television commercials are often memorized by young children. Blind children should be given the braille corresponding to memorized material and, in this way, be introduced to the "feeling" of continuous braille reading.

Summary

This chapter was written on the premise that in the areas related to reading readiness blind children develop differently than sighted children. Parents and pre-school teachers need to make more deliberate efforts to develop and refine sensory abilities in blind children than would be necessary with sighted children. The environment must be brought to blind children in an organized, consistent, and meaningful way. Concepts must be taught in a similar fashion. Understanding of basic concepts must stem from a child's personal interaction with the environment, rather than from rote memorization of verbal definitions. Finally, exposure to the braille medium must occur as early in the lives of blind children as exposure to print occurs for sighted children. Not only must pre-school blind children become aware of braille as a means of communication, they must also have enough positive experiences with it to be sufficiently motivated to learn how to understand it.

References

Barraga, N. *Increased visual behavior in low vision children.* New York: American Foundation for the Blind, 1964.

Cratty, B. *Movement and spatial awareness in blind children and youth.* Springfield, Illinois: Charles C Thomas, 1971.

Cutsforth, T. *The blind child in school and society.* New York: American Foundation for the Blind, 1951.

Fraiberg, S. Parallel and divergent patterns in blind and sighted infants. *Psychoanalytic Study of the Child,* 1968, **23**, 264-300.

Fraiberg, S. *Insights from the blind—comparative studies of blind and sighted infants.* New York: Basic Books, Inc., 1977.

Frisina, D. Hearing disorders. In N.G. Haring and R.L. Schiefelbusch (Eds.) *Methods in special education.* New York: McGraw-Hill, 1967.

Foulke, E. Non-visual communication. *International Journal for the Education of the Blind,* 1968, **18**, 77-78.

Foulke, E. Reading by listening. *Education of the Visually Handicapped,* 1969, **1**, 79-81.

Hammill, D., & Crandell, J. Implications of tactile-kinesthetic ability in visually handicapped children. *Education of the Visually Handicapped,* 1968, **1**, 65-69.

Hanninen, K. *Teaching the visually handicapped.* Columbus, Ohio: Charles Merrill Publishing Company, 1975.

Harrell, L. Developmental levels and suggested learning activities. A special report compiled for the Clearinghouse Depository for Handicapped Students of California, May 1977.

Lowenfeld, B. *The visually handicapped child in school.* New York: John Day Company, 1973.

Lydon, W., & McGraw, M. *Concept development for visually handicapped children.* New York: American Foundation for the Blind, 1973.

Miller, G. The magical number seven, plus or minus two: Some limits on our capacity for processing information. In N.G. Slamesha (Ed.) *Human learning and memory.* New York: Oxford University Press, 1967.

Révész, G. *Psychology and art of the blind.* New York: Longmans, Green, 1950.

Zweibelson, I., & Barg, C. Concept development of blind children. *New Outlook for the Blind,* 1967, **61**(7), 218.

Chapter IV
Activities for Teaching Braille More Efficiently at the Beginning Level

Incorporation of Rapid Reading Principles

It is the purpose of this chapter to suggest how rapid reading principles might be incorporated into the teaching of beginning braille reading. "Beginning reading" here is meant to include instruction through grade three. Regardless of age, newly blinded readers learning braille, and consequently reading at these levels, might also be helped by activities in this chapter. Studies of braille reading strongly suggest that frequently observed undesirable braille reading behaviors may be prevented if the initial instruction in braille reading focuses primarily upon good reading habits, rather than on decoding skills (Bloom, 1974; Douglas and Mangold, 1975). Once the mechanics of braille reading are mastered, the student can devote all of his energies toward more complex skills and perform at a higher level of reading accuracy. Through the application of rapid reading techniques, the mechanics of braille reading can be mastered more efficiently (Umsted, 1972; Wallace, 1973; McBride, 1974; Olson, 1975).

The incorporation of rapid reading principles into beginning braille instruction would by no means constitute a total "reading approach," but it can serve as an adjunct to any of the approaches mentioned in Chapter One. This chapter discusses how this might be done by breaking down the reading process into various skill areas. A certain amount of overlap cannot be avoided, since the process of reading is extremely complex and does not truly lend itself to a rigid analysis of this sort. Since many braille readers are mainstreamed into classes with sighted children, the final portion of this chapter gives suggestions to the resource or itinerant teacher for facilitating carryover of braille reading skills to the child's studies in the regular classroom.

Attitude Development

A child's first impression of braille is extremely important. Various suggestions were made in Chapter Three for fostering good attitudes and providing pre-school exposure to braille. There is a definite need to continue this effort when the child starts school or begins actual braille instruction.

The beginning braille reader will need a large amount of support from an individual knowledgeable about braille, such as a resource or itinerant vision teacher, a community volunteer, an older student, or a parent. Whoever this person is, the following activities are suggested for encouraging a positive attitude toward beginning braille instruction:

1) Label the child's school surroundings with Grade 2 braille. This might include his desk, book shelves, books, locker, brailler, miscellaneous school supplies, the teacher's desk, wastebasket, pencil sharpener, and bulletin board. Physically guide the child to the location of each label and read it to him.

2) Provide good models of braille reading. If you are not a tactual braille reader, an outside resource person might be invited in during "book sharing time." In a mainstreamed setting, sighted children would also benefit from such a demonstration.

3) Demonstrate how braille is read by placing the child's hands over yours as you move both hands down a page. Discuss with the child examples of times braille might be used in everyday living.

4) Read to the child books that have both print and braille in them. Have the child "follow along" even though he is not decoding the braille in the beginning.

5) Have the child dictate to you a few short sentences describing an experience that is important to him. Braille the sentences for him to "read" back to you. You might also braille songs, television commercials, or nursery rhymes that the child has committed to memory.

6) Make the child's first braille books interesting for him to explore. Make the pages a different shape occasionally (e.g., round, triangular, tree-shaped, animal-shaped). The shape may actually give the child a "clue" as to what the book is about. You can also make the cover tactually interesting by covering it with fabrics, small objects, string designs, etc. You may wish to make this into an art project.

7) Braille printed items that sighted children in a regular classroom would enjoy examining. Examples of such things would be calendars, lunch menus, special program agendas, and notes to parents.

8) Do not place the beginning braille reader in a regular classroom reading group until he has the skills to "keep up" and feel successful. For the first several weeks of the school year you may need to schedule him out of the regular classroom (if he's in a mainstreamed setting) to receive intensive help learning to read braille. Before placing him in a reading group with print readers, he should be able to read approximately as fast as most children in the group. He should also know how to locate stories through the use of the table of contents and to locate page numbers.

Mechanical Skills

Outlined below are a number of mechanical skills that are unique to braille reading. These skills must be well developed before placing any emphasis on decoding of braille words, phrases or sentences.

Finger dexterity/wrist flexibility.

1) Involve the child in sorting and stacking activities. Begin with large, familiar objects such as boxes and toys. Gradually introduce smaller objects such as nails and paper clips.

2) Provide beads for stringing, with the sizes becoming progressively smaller.

3) Give the child braille paper to punch. Have him "sew" with yarn through the punched holes. Additional art projects that encourage fine finger manipulations are paper weaving, paper folding, cutting and pasting.

4) Collect various sizes of jars with screw-type covers. Have the child sort small objects and put them into the jars. Nuts and bolts of various sizes also provide similar kinds of movement.

5) Combine teaching of math concepts and counting with fine motor activities. One example might include having the child attach pinch clothespins on a hanger for simple counting purposes. Each fine motor task should be accomplished with each hand separately as well as both hands together.

6) Tape record directions to some of the above activities so that the child gets practice in working independently. Teaching him to operate a cassette recorder will also help him develop fine motor skills needed for reading braille.

Hand Movements/Finger Positions

1) Demonstrate correct finger position to the child. You may wish to use a book or the edge of a ruler to help the child learn the correct curvature for his fingers.

2) Make some simulated reading materials to help teach hand movement. These simulated materials might consist of popsicle sticks or yarn glued to braille paper. Thread lines made with a sewing machine or lines of a single repeated braille symbol may also be used. The purpose for not using real braille reading material at this point is to remove the child's focus from the geometry of the braille symbols so that he can concentrate on the more generalized skill of efficient hand movement and finger placement.

3) Introduce to the child terminology that will help him remember that each finger has a function. For example, there are "lead fingers" and "detectives." Even though two or three fingers may take major responsibility for reading, all other fingers are needed for verification or "checking up" on these lead fingers. Children very quickly become comfortable using just a single finger; teachers must resist the temptation to allow this. Although the student's short-range efficiency appears better with one hand, his long-range efficiency will suffer if both hands are not used.

4) Demonstrate smooth, independent movements of the hands to the student. Place his hands over yours in doing this.

5) Mangold (1977) advocates tracking double-spaced lines of repetitious braille to establish rapid, smooth hand movements. To assist a student in moving from line to line, horizontal or vertical (tactual) line guides are suggested. When smooth tracking is accomplished with a single hand, two-handed tracking is introduced through the use of double spaced two columned braille. The student is directed to read across the line with both hands until he comes to a vertical line. At this point, his left hand is to return to the beginning of the next line, while his right hand finishes the previous line. The tactual vertical line separating the two columns of braille is then replaced by several blank spaces. Illustration of these exercises are provided in ink print on pages 39–42. A direct excerpt from the Mangold *Developmental Program of Tactile Perception and Braille Letter Recognition* is provided to assist teachers in preparing these exercises and in instructing children to use them. It should be noted that no exercises should be considered complete in itself. As was described in Chapter Three, the Mangold Program provides lessons that are carefully sequenced and based upon criteria for mastery.

It must be remembered that individual children will develop their own best tracking patterns. Thus, it is important to encourage experimentation with respect to how the left hand returns to the beginning of a new line or at what point it returns to find the next line. Some excellent braille readers go down to the new line at the half-way point on the old line and track backwards over the new line to its beginning. Many of these readers report picking up some information as they do this backward reading.

6) Illustrate what is meant by "margin" (top, bottom, left, right). Give the child practice tracking from one margin to another.

7) Teach the child about spacing and paragraphing by using repetitious braille in the format of real braille.

8) Have the child count the number of idented lines he finds as he tracks rapidly down a page.

Light Finger Touch

1) Place checkers on braille graph paper and have the child practice touching them so lightly that they do not move outside of the squares.

2) Have the child rub his fingertips in colored chalk and then track across pages of old magazines to see how long he can track making continuous contact before he runs out of color. The teacher will have to tell the student how well he is progressing in this task. The student will feel more involved if he records and charts his progress.

3) Demonstrate how lightly braille should be touched. Have the child practice this, while giving him praise for making light continous contact without scrubbing the dots.

**Double Spaced c's With Vertical Line Guide
For the Left Hand**

**Double Space c's With Vertical Midline Guide
For Return Sweep**

Double Spaced g's With Diagonal Line Guide
For Return Sweeps To Next Line

:: :: :: :: :: :: :: :: :: :: :: :: :: :: :: :: :: :: :: ::

:: :: :: :: :: :: :: :: :: :: :: :: :: :: :: :: :: :: :: ::

:: :: :: :: :: :: :: :: :: :: :: :: :: :: :: :: :: :: :: ::

:: :: :: :: :: :: :: :: :: :: :: :: :: :: :: :: :: :: :: ::

Double Spaced c's For Teaching Variable
Lengths of Lines on a Page

•• •• •• •• •• •• •• •• •• •• •• •• •• •• •• ••

•• •• •• •• •• •• •• ••

•• •• •• •• •• •• •• •• •• •• •• •• ••

•• •• •• •• •• •• •• •• •• •• •• •• •• •• •• ••

Excerpted from the Mangold Developmental Program of Tactile Perception and Braille Letter Recognition (Print page 18, braille page 17)

Braille **LESSON 1**
Page 17   This exercise will teach a student to use his hands in-dependently. Some students are ready to use their hands in-dependently as soon as they begin reading braille. Other students use both hands together for a long time before they can easily use their hands independently. If on page 17 the student becomes frustrated, or begins to skip lines remove page 17 through 22 and place them at the end of lesson 14 for later use.

Use the following instructions when you use braille page 17-22.

Direct the student to track across the short lines with both hands together and go over all of the lines on the left side of the page first,then the right side of the page. Now have the student go back to the top of the page. Think about the two short lines as being one long line all the way across the page. Have the student track the left short line with both hands, stop at the vertical line, finish tracking the right side with his right hand only. Do every line the same way. Allow the student to use this method on the criterion test if he wishes.

aaaaaaaaaaaa	aaaaaaaaaaaa
cccccccccccc	aaaaaaaaaaaa
cccccccccccc	aaaaaaaaaaaa
gggggggggggg	cccccccccccc
gggggggggggg	cccccccccccc
gggggggggggg	cccccccccccc
gggggggggggg	cccccccccccc
gggggggggggg	cccccccccccc
############	aaaaaaaaaaaa
############	bbbbbbbbbbbb
############	bbbbbbbbbbbb

Double Space Two Column Repetitious Braille
Independent Hand Movements

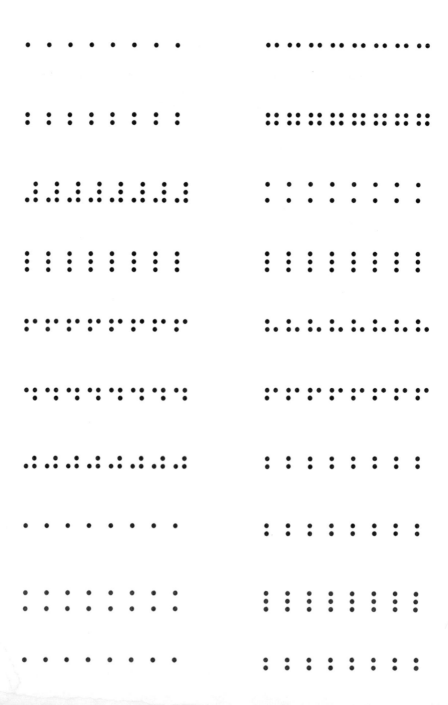

4) Construct a homemade tachistoscope for the child. One way to do this would be to braille repetitious symbols on Western Union ticker tape. Pulls the tape beneath the child's fingers as he places them over the edge of a book or a ruler. The purpose of this exercise is to see how "high" he can hold his fingers and still detect the presence or absence of braille symbols. When you are ready to work on discrimination of the symbols, this exercise can be used again to pick out the symbol that is "different."

Tactile Perception/Discrimination

Once the mechanical skills are mastered, the child is ready to sharpen his tactile perception and to recognize differences among braille configurations. There seems to be no "right way" to introduce this phase of instruction. Some teachers introduce the braille alphabet first. Others introduce whole words in the beginning. Most teachers, however, modify their approach according to the needs of individual children. My personal bias is that some language experience stories ought to constitute a part of every child's initial exposure to braille. By several readings of material the child himself has dictated, he begins to make associations between symbols and their meanings. The teacher may wish to control the vocabulary that is studied to avoid use of lower cell contractions—or even contractions of any kind.

For those teachers choosing to introduce alphabet letters first, it might be good to make a list of words commonly used in a kindergarten or primary setting. For example, color words are referred to with high frequency at this level. Some of the color words (blue, orange, purple, black) contain no contractions and might be an appropriate list with which to start. If the resource teacher (or any support person) makes a tactual drawing within which the blind child can color, these drawings can be labeled with the color words; the child's crayons would also need to be labeled. Large, triangular crayons work very well with blind children since they do not roll off desks easily and have a large enough surface to attach a label. Tactual drawings can be made several ways. A quick method for producing a tactual outline is on a screenboard. A screenboard can be made by attaching a piece of metal screening to the back of a flannel board; the edges should be bound with masking tape. When one writes with crayon (placed on top of the screen), the lines can be detected tactually.

Regardless of the approach each teacher chooses when introducing meaning to braille symbols, care must be taken with respect to description and timing. Symbols which are reversible pairs (i and e; r and w; of and with; er and q; ou and t; sh and m; u and ing) ought never be referred to as "reversals" of each other. Additionally, they should never be introduced together; one of each pair needs to be mastered before the other is learned. Although it is helpful for children to know that the six dots in a braille cell are numbered, it is my opinion that these numbers should not be recalled every time the symbol is encountered. In other words, the student needs to learn the geometric shape of each braille cell without having to memorize the dot numbers comprising each shape.

My collaborator on this book, Dr. Sally Mangold, has developed and field tested a program for teaching tactile perception and braille letter recognition. Dr. Mangold has found throughout her years as a resource teacher that pre-school blind children do not get the exposure to left-right tracking or to letter recognition that sighted children receive. Her program is based upon a precision teaching model and is described in some depth below:

The Mangold Developmental Program of Tactile Perception and Braille Letter Recognition.

A study was conducted by Dr. Mangold, to determine the extent to which a developmental program of tactile perception and braille letter recognition might significantly decrease scrubbing, backtracking, and letter reversal errors of braille readers. The model program required 12 to 16 weeks to administer, depending upon the abilities of each of the thirty subjects (ages 5 to 15 years).

The sequenced exercises that make up this program are designed to teach the mechanics of braille reading—the characteristic hand positions and movement techniques typical of good two-handed braille readers. The arduous task of decoding abstract symbols becomes much easier if the reader has already mastered tracking, skimming, identification of like and different, light finger touch, and left to right movement of the hands.

The proponents of precision teaching believe that a student who overlearns a skill will incorporate it so thoroughly in his repertoire of knowledge that when he moves on, he will not confuse items that are similar to newly introduced material (e.g., e [••] and i [••] in braille). He will also expend little energy performing an overlearned skill and will consequently have greater energy available to apply to mastery of the new skill.

Data analysis revealed that, as hypothesized, the experimental subjects demonstrated significantly fewer errors in tactile perception, braille letter recognition, and undesirable backtracking and scrubbing. This was true of the subjects who were new braille readers as well as of those subjects who had a history of reading difficulties.

Precision teaching assessment techniques used throughout the study resulted in the establishment of criteria for 19 subskills of tactile perception and braille letter recognition. If a student can perform a particular task at the rate recommended, it is suggested that he skip worksheets teaching that skill and proceed to a higher level of difficulty. Practice worksheets are included after each criterion test for use by those students who have not yet mastered the skill under consideration.

Precision teaching is not a new teaching approach. It is designed to supplement an existing program and can be used by teachers who have a wide variety of teaching styles. It has four parts: 1) Identify a skill to be mastered; 2) The skill is broken down into subskills by the teacher; 3) The student is assessed by the teacher on these subskills to ascertain his current rate of response; 4) A daily one-minute timing on each skill designated by the teacher is done on three consecutive days to determine the student's potential rate of progress. An example: A student might be assessed on his ability to read and say a lower case letter. The letters are presented in a horizontal format and written in a random order. The recommended mastery of this skill is 70 letters per minute. A student should improve at least 30% on a skill during a ten-day period. Many students will improve more than this. If a student falls below the 30% improvement level, it is probably because the skill being taught is too difficult. An easier task should be substituted for the current one.

The Mangold Developmental Program is not designed to be a complete program of reading instruction. It should be used for only that portion of reading instruction devoted to tactile perception and braille letter recognition. It most schools, this would constitute about one-third of the reading period. Concept development, auditory discrimination, and phonetic skills are also vital elements in a comprehensive reading instruction program.

The decision as to the appropriateness of the developmental program for a particular student must be based upon knowledge of the student's overall level of functioning, his ability to comprehend language, attend to a task, and manipulate read objects.

The purpose of the Mangold Development Program is not only to produce students who read well but to produce students who *love* to read.

The 29 lessons of Tactile Perception and Braille Letter Recognition include criteria tests and worksheets that promote mastery of the following skills:

1) Tracking from left to right across like symbols that follow closely without a space between them.

2) Tracking from left to right across unlike symbols that follow closely without a space between them.

3) Tracking from left to right across like symbols that have one or two blank spaces between them.

4) Tracking from left to right across unlike symbols that have one or two blank spaces between them.

5) Tracking from top to bottom over like symbols that follow closely without a space between them.

6) Tracking from top to bottom over unlike symbols that follow closely without a space between them.

7) Tracking from top to bottom over like symbols that have one blank space between them.

8) Tracking from top to bottom over unlike symbols that have one blank space between them.

9) Identifying two geometric shapes as being the same or different.

10) Identifying two braille symbols as being the same or different.

11) Identifying two braille symbols as being the same or different when they are preceded and followed by a solid line.

12) Identifying the one symbol which is different within a line of like symbols, using the letter "l" and the letter "c".

13) Identifying the one symbol that is different within a line of like symbols using a variety of braille symbols for different lines.

14) Identifying the one symbol that is different within a group of three symbols, two of which are identical.

Lessons 15 through 29 introduce the letters of the alphabet in the following sequence: c   g   l   d   y   a   b   s   w   p   o   k   r   m   e   h   n   x   z   f   u   t   q   i   v   j.

Reinforcement games which use the skills that have been mastered are scattered throughout the program. These games along with suggested achievement charting have proven to maintain a high level of student motivation. For more information on this program write to: Exceptional Teaching Aids, 20102 Woodbine Avenue, Castro Valley, California 94546.

Kinesthetic Skills

When teaching rapid reading to experienced readers, it become essential to break bad mechanical habits. A technique for breaking these habits is "unreading" or reading for no comprehension. The value of this technique is to establish the "kinesthetic" or internal feeling of reading smoothly and rapidly. When applied to the teaching of beginning reading, it would involve much "pretend reading." The child should be given the opportunity to "read" material that is memorized before had has learned to decode braille symbols. This kind of activity should be scattered throughout the time period in which discriminatory skills are being developed as well. For some children, timing and charting the number of pages covered in one minute's time is a useful technique.

Decoding Skills

In this section, decoding will be referred to in its narrowest sense—that of developing awareness of the sound-symbol relationship. While decoding of symbols cannot be completely isolated from comprehension, skill in decoding is nonetheless being enhanced when the student uses context, structural clues, experiential background, sight vocabulary and spelling patterns to help to understand the string of symbols he is touching.

Some teachers approach decoding analytically. For instance, they have students note similarities among sight words such as "mother," "milk" and "man" when teaching the sound of "m." Other teachers prefer a synthetic approach that looks at sounds in isolation. These sounds are subsequently pronounced in rapid succession so that the student understands how words are built (blended). Regardless of the approach, the following suggestions may be helpful in working with braille readers.

1) The *Ginn Reading Series* provides good practice in auditory discrimination (Level 1) as well as decoding (Levels 2 and 3). If another reading series is being used in a mainstreamed setting, the resource or itinerant teacher may wish to use these books for extra drill purposes.

2) Braille symbols that are reversible pairs should never be introduced together.

3) Short passages of the child's reading series can be taped so that he is able to hear the sounds being pronounced as his fingers pass over the braille symbols.

4) When introducing or drilling sounds, objects that are familiar to the child should be substituted for picture-type stimuli. Below is a list of beginning consonant sounds, long and short vowel sounds with one or more objects to use for each:

Consonants
b - ball, bean, book
c - cup, cap, comb
d - doll, drum, dish
f - feather, football, fan
g - gun, glasses, gum
h - horn, hook
j - jack-in-the-box, jar, jump rope
k - key, kite
l - light bulb, lace
m - mitten, magnet, match
n - nail
p - paper, pencil, pen
q - quarter, quack (from rubber
    duck)
r - rock, rubber bank, rule
s - sucker, sock, sandpaper

Long Vowels
a - tape, cane
e - peanut, leaf
i - dime
u - ruler

Short Vowels
a - can, apple
e - pen
i - pin
o - top
u - sucker

5) An independent activity for students to do would be to match objects that have "like beginning sounds," "like ending sounds," or "like middle sounds."

6) Taped instructions to matching exercises foster independence. In addition to matching objects, as in #5 above, the student may be asked to match brailled words to objects or brailled words to each other.

7) When asking students to do matching exercises, provide compartments for them to pair or group items. If the items are small, muffin tins work very well. For larger objects, several cardboard cheese boxes can be stapled together.

8) As the student encounters verbal symbols for the words he already knows and uses as part of his listening and speaking vocabulary, he is learning to associate a particular symbol with a known word. He may notice that when he says a particular word, it is tactually a "short" one. The teacher can facilitate this use of configuration clues by pointing out the shape of braille words that the child encounters. For the beginning braille reader, it might be best if uncontracted words are used because the length of the word will then be more directly related to the length of its sound.

9) Like sighted print readers, braille readers require daily drill and practice in decoding. It is good if the teacher keeps a record of the student's errors each day, so that she has a better idea of readiness to "move on."

Vocabulary Development

During the primary grades, major attention is given to developing a sight vocabulary and the word-analysis skills that promote independent reading. The third-level reader often serves as a transition from an emphasis on decoding "new" words to a greater concern about developing the meanings of words. From then on, one of the major objectives of reading instruction is helping children to build reading vocabularies that are wide ranging, rich and accurate.

No attempt will be made here to cover the innumerable ways of enhancing vocabulary development. Rather, a few ideas will be described with accompanying adaptations for the braille reader.

1) Writing experience stories is a good way to promote vocabulary development. Words that have been confined to the child's listening vocabulary may be transferred to his speaking vocabulary and ultimately to his reading vocabulary. The major advantage of using experience stories is that they are motivating. Students see words that are meaningful to them because they describe the children's own experiences. For the child who has not mastered decoding skills, it is still possible to read through reliance on memory. The major disadvantage of using experience stories is that there is no control over vocabulary used. We know that some contractions are more difficult to recognize than others (i.e. lower cell contractions, two cell contractions). To overcome this problem, the teacher must guide the selection of words for experience stories. This is done by suggesting experiences to write about and by phrasing questions in a way that elicits specific vocabulary words. In addition to choosing words that are easier to recognize tactually, the teacher must be aware of words the child is encountering in his classroom reading

series; these words can be drilled and practiced during the time spent with the resource or itinerant teacher.

2) The resource or itinerant teacher can supplement the classroom teacher's vocabulary-building efforts by taking note of the pictures the basal reading series contains. If at all feasible, the blind child should be given the opportunity to "experience" the activities portrayed in these pictures. This may involve giving the information to the child's parents through a phone call, meeting or letter.

3) Verify that the blind child understands the meanings of words. Ask him to demonstrate his understanding through body gestures.

4) Help the student to categorize words. Begin with having him identify names or "do" words. Additional categories might be animals, things to eat, things to wear, and so forth. If the words are brailled on flashcards, they can be placed into sectioned boxes, tied or clipped to a string, or pinned on a line. Regular classroom teachers may develop category games in which the child spins a dial and has to name a word fitting the category indicated when the dial stops. The resource or itinerant teacher can facilitate the blind student's participation in such games by brailling labels for the gameboard or the cards used.

5) Present new words to the student in context rather than in isolation. Have the student construct his own notebook or dictionary of new words. Instead of writing a definition of the word, a sentence might be written beside the word, illustrating its meaning through context.

6) When transcribing story books to braille, vary the shape of the pages and the cover. Sighted children are attracted to books largely by attractive and interesting book jackets. We cannot expect the braille reader to be enthusiastic about identical rectangular sheets of braille paper.

7) To further develop vocabulary, the regular classroom teacher may use rhyming exercises, and the study of roots, prefixes, and suffixes. Most of these exercises will require the resource or itinerant teacher to transcribe print to braille or record exercises on tape. The format of some of the print materials may also have to be changed. Guidelines for these format changes are discussed in depth at the end of this chapter.

Comprehension Skills

The development of adequate comprehension skills is a very complex process. Students must be able not only to understand what the author is saying (literal comprehension) but must also be able to infer meaning (inferential comprehension), and make a judgment about what is read (evaluation comprehension). It is also important for students to enjoy and appreciate the literary qualities of a story.

Comprehension skills can be taught in numerous ways. Regardless of the approach used, it is at first essential for reading material to be kept interesting and brief. In addition to this general suggestion, several more specific ideas are outlined pages 50-51:

1)When working on comprehension skills, allow the student to read in a quiet area, apart from a group. Gradually build tolerance for noise and distraction so that the student is able to function independently in a classroom with several children.

2) As with vocabulary building, the student needs first-hand experiences in order to relate to the braille words on a page. Many concepts can be developed through exposure to real objects that the student can handle.

3) When the blind child is reading, encourage him to use tactual, auditory and kinesthetic imagery. Ask him questions about what he smells, feels, tastes while reading a particular story. If the student has once been sighted, he may also be able to conjure up visual images of things described in his reading. When first working on this skill, have the student listen to tapes so that you can monitor his progress. Stop the tape occasionally and discuss what a word, phrase or sentence causes the student to see, taste, hear or feel.

4) Configuration or shape clues were discussed under decoding skills (p. 46–47). The student should be encouraged to use this technique when reading for comprehension as well. One way to begin working on this is to develop an automatic vocabulary of sight words, since a relatively small number of words make up a high proportion of most reading material. The Dolch Word List is a commercially available list of sight words. These may be brailled on flash cards and used for drill. In addition to commonly appearing words, frequently occurring letter combinations might also be studied for their unique shapes.

5) Closely related to using shape clues to enhance comprehension skills, is the use of structural clues. The resource or itinerant teacher must point out word beginnings, endings, spelling patterns and letter repetitions which will give additional clues to the reader. By brailling sentences with missing letters, word parts, and words, the teacher can illustrate the use of structural clues.

6) Brailled exercises with deleted words and phrases can be used to practice the use of context clues. Another activity that encourages the use of context is scanning a page rapidly to pick up two or three words. Further re-readings of the same page helps to fill in missing details and provides more practice in using context clues.

7) Make frequent checks of comprehension. Do not rely on "factual" questions but ask how the child feels about what he has read, for example: 1) What happened in the story that happened to you? 2) How did you feel when you read about _____? 3) How would you change this story to make it better? [See Appendix A for further illustrations of non-factual questions.]

8) Sighted children rely heavily on pictures for understanding printed words on a page. The blind child can gain some of this type of information during silent reading periods by listening to tape recorded descriptions of the pictures in a particular story. By using earphones, he avoids interrupting others reading silently in the same room.

9) Give the braille reader opportunities to read a variety of material. As he progresses through school he needs to be exposed to poetry, fiction, descriptive material, editorials, and directions (such as in recipes).

Flexibility Skills

While we certainly want children to read smoothly and rapidly, it is even more important for them to be flexible readers. They should be able to vary their reading speed according to the material encountered and the reasons for reading that material. Teachers must therefore deliberately introduce reading activities with some direction for *how* the children should be reading. This implies giving readers a variety of materials on which to practice and giving them specific purposes for reading. The following are suggestions for teaching scanning, skimming, and reflective reading.

Scan Reading. The purpose of "scan reading" is to locate a specific item or items on a page without attempting to understand the context in which they appear. Tables of content, indexes, telephone directories, and dictionaries are good materials for practicing this skill. Although it is not practical to think in terms of a braille telephone directory, it is realistic to think that a braille reader may have a page or two of telephone numbers to scan. Columns of numbers can be used as exercises in "looking at" numbers. Children often enjoy making a time game of scanning; this may even extend to having them take open book examinations. Before beginning the search for an item on a page, the child should be told to imagine how that item will "feel" under his fingers when he locates it. Expecting the item to "stand out" tactually facilitates scan reading.

Skim Reading. The reason one "skim reads" is to get an overview of something. This implies putting bits and pieces together to get the "whole picture." Tables of content, introductions, titles, subtitles, summaries and topic sentences of individual paragraphs are appropriate for teaching skimming. Below are more specific techniques for introducing this type of reading:

1) When giving a reading assignment, give the student general questions to answer. Have him practice formulating his own questions based on book titles, chapter headings, etc.

2) Identify and drill for rapid recognition of "sign-post" words that signal a continuation of thought. Examples of sign-post words are: and, also, likewise, moreover, furthermore. Additionally, identify and drill for rapid recognition of "turn-about" words that change the direction of thought. Examples of words like this are: but, yet, nevertheless, despite. It should be noted here that the beginning reader may not encounter some of these examples; the teacher should drill those which are appropriate to the material the child is reading.

4) As previously mentioned under the development of comprehension

skills, have the child practice rapid, automatic recognition of common words. A word list such as the Dolch should be brailled on flashcards and in vertical and horizontal lists.

5) Set rate and comprehension goals for material that is being read. Have each child time and charge himself regularly. The timing procedure can be made an independent activity if the teacher simply records "go" and "stop" on a tape at 30-second or 60-second intervals.

6) As with scan reading, open book examinations will facilitate the practice of reading for main ideas.

7) Reinforce reading for the "main idea" through writing activities. Discuss logical organization and sequencing of ideas initially. Follow this discussion with the direction to write sample paragraphs that are "easy" vs. "hard" to skim for the main idea.

9) A good skimming technique was described under the development of comprehensions skills. It was suggested that students gain practice in using context clues by rapidly re-reading a single page several items. This technique might be called "bits and pieces" reading because initially the student is asked to pick out only two or three words per page. As he re-reads the same page, he picks up additional words to fill in missing details.

Reading Style Development

How a child sits (or stands), holds a book, and moves his hands determines his braille reading "style." A broader definition of reading style might also include desire for quiet or ambient noise, presence or absence of subvocalization, or movements of other body parts while reading. Chapter Two mentioned some reading styles that appear to be superior, in that most "good" braille readers use them. Nevertheless, the important thing to keep in mind is that reading style is highly individual and to determine what reading style best suits a particular child, he must be encouraged to experiment. Listed below are some ways teachers can foster this experimentation:

1) Provide a variety of reading environments: a) vary the noise level; b) introduce chair/table combinations that differ in height; c) allow children to sit on floor cushions occasionally for reading.

2) Demonstrate ways to hold a braille book: a) Parallel vs. slight angle; b) use of book prop; c) use of the lap.

3) Demonstrate ways to move one's hands independently across a braille page: Help the student experiment with innovative ways of moving his hands.

4) Help the child reduce subvocalizations: a) Place a pencil between his teeth while reading; b) have the student chew gum while reading.

5) Encourage children to discuss their braille reading styles with each other.

Memorization of Braille Code Rules

Those of us who learned the braille code by sight remember with distaste memorizing the rules for using it. Fortunately, blind children learn these rules incidentally as they read braille. Although teachers may wish to discuss a particular rule when the child is writing braille, there is little need to dwell on rules when teaching braille reading.

Carryover Skills: Special Setting to the Regular Classroom

Most of the suggestions given for the above skill areas were geared toward the resource or itinerant teacher. Nonetheless, the regular classroom teacher also must be conversant with work the blind child does outside her classroom. Furthermore, knowledge of the role of the resource or itinerant teacher, helps the regular classroom teacher cooperate more effectively, and thus provide better carryover. Following are a few ways in which all teachers working with the braille reader might truly make this a "team" effort.

Regular Classroom Teacher. The regular classroom teacher needs to plan ahead with respect to skill objectives and materials. By outlining the objectives of her reading program and giving the resource of itinerant persons a list of texts, worksheets, and tests ahead of time, the braille reading child will be able to "keep up"; with his sighted peers. This kind of cooperation also gives the resource or itinerant teacher time to transcribe or tape materials and enables her to do supplementary tutoring in the skill areas when it is needed. These teachers will have to decide how much "lead time" is needed for transcribing, recording or ordering materials. A great deal will depend upon the availability of volunteer or paid transcribers and tapists. A resource or itinerant teacher working alone cannot be expected to accomplish these tasks in a few short days. As soon as the classroom placement of a blind child is known, the vision teacher and the regular classroom teacher should meet to discuss materials needed for the upcoming school years.

Resource or Itinerant Teacher. It is helpful if a good relationship can be established with the regular classroom teacher during the spring preceding the blind child's entry to school in the fall. It is vitally important for the resource or itinerant teacher to be familiar with the regular classroom's reading curriculum and routine. When the regular classroom teacher feels comfortable with the vision teacher as a person, she is more likely to allow observation of her classroom without fear of "being critically judged." A regular system of communication must be established between these teachers. This might mean setting up a particular day of the week or time of the day for conferring together. When this is impossible, it may involve agreeing upon a place for picking up and delivering transcribed or taped material. Following are a few suggestion for the resource or itinerant teacher that will help facilitate the use of braille in the regular classroom.

1) *Certain materials should be available to the regular classroom teacher at the beginning of the year.* These are:

a) Braille versions of the first readers to be used

b) Braille versions of the first workbook pages to be used

c) Braille wordlists or flashcards of vocabulary being introduced to the readers. Interline the flashcards with manuscript writing so that sighted children can read them. Clip off one corner of each flashcards, so that the student can tell which is the right side up

d) Braille versions of school bulletins, menus, calendars (on-going)

e) Push pin board with push pins (approximately 11″ by 11″ particle board covered with contact paper)

f) Non-slip pad for placement of worksheets and for quieting the braille writer's sound

2) *Double space all material that is transcribed from the first reader; double space all worksheets that require a braille response on them.* There is as much as a half-line discrepancy among braille writers; by double spacing the child's worksheets, he can roll them into the braille writer to record an answer without writing over something else.

3) *Transcribe material having picture content according to the reason for inclusion of the picture.*

a) If the picture does not enhance the meaning of the text and is in fact unnecessary, omit reference to it.

b) If the picture consist of simple changes, a tracing wheel replica can be substituted. It is also possible to duplicate outlines in yarn, string or electrician's narrow tape; these outlines may or may not be Thermo-formed, depending upon the need for durability.

c) If complex figures are used in print but are not needed for conveying the concept, substitute simple geometric shapes and braille characters. EXAMPLE: Choose the ones that are different.

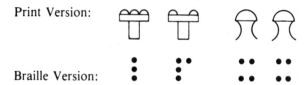

Print Version:

Braille Version:

d) If the picture enhances the words content, tape record a description of the picture.

e) If the picture demands understanding of detailed pictorial content, use objects or models supplemented by individual tutoring.
EXAMPLE: Learn the exact location of a body part
                 Interpret differences in two objects

f) If the picture is meant to arouse interest in a story or give a mere "clue" to its content, make a tactual substitution for the picture.

EXAMPLE: Feather = story about a duck or bird
Shoelace = story about shoes

4) *When transcribing print materials to braille, it is often necessary to alter the format for ease of reading in braille.*

a) Directions for completing a worksheet should always appear at the top of a braille page, regardless of where they are found in print. The reason for this is that braille versions of single print pages may be two to three pages in length; the directions may thus occur on the second or third page, causing confusion to the braille reader.

b) A long dash (four dots 3-6) is used in braille to indicate a blank for insertion of a braille answer. The student should be instructed to braille his answer after the blank, instead of above it, as is usually seen in print. This practice reduces the need to continuously roll the braille paper up and down to read and respond to the questions. Two spaces more than those needed for the correct answer should be provided to the right of the long dash.

c) Display word, phrase or sentence items on multiple-choice questions horizontally rather than vertically. This also reduces the number of times the student has to roll the paper up and down in the braille writer. It is similarly helpful if the response choices are brailled in advance of each question.

d) When print instructions on a worksheet require single and double underlines to indicate correct choices, a line of c's can be used to make a single underline in braille; a line of x's would give the appearance of a double underline.

e) On phonics exercises that give pictures as clues to decoding a choice of words, the stimulus word for the picture should be placed on tape. The child then chooses the brailled word on the basis of the auditory stimulus.

5) *A push-pin board and push pins may be the intermediate form of response to a braille worksheet; brailled responses recorded from the push-pin board should then be interlined with print by the resource or itinerant teacher.*

6) *Print materials that are tape recorded must be recorded with pauses.* A minimum of three seconds between directions and between individual questions should be left on the tape made for a braille student. This time lag allows him to turn the recorder off before brailling a response and to turn it back on to listen to the next item.

7) *When transcribing programmed material for the braille reader, the direction of the binding may have to be changed.* The textual material and questions can be bound on the left, just as print materials are bound. The self-checking key, however, is best used by the braille reader if it is bound on the right. The transcriber should make certain that the spacing of the questions matches the spacing of the answers.

8) *Transcribed materials should be used for supplementary tutoring whenever feasible.* Materials brailled for the regular classroom can often be used by the resource or itinerant teacher for multiple purposes in a tutoring session. Below are some examples:

a) Put a push-pin in all the words beginning with the sound of "m"
b) Put a push-pin in all the words that rhyme with "cat"
c) Braille a list of all the words that name things to wear
d) Count the number of *(insert symbol child confuses)* on this page.

References

Bammen, H., Dawson, N. and McGovern, J. *Fundamentals of basic reading instruction.* New York: McKay, 1973.

Bloom, B. Time and learning. *American Psychologist,* 1974, **29** (9), 682-688.

Douglas, S. and Mangold, S., Precision teaching of visually impaired students. *Education of the Visually Handicapped*, 1975, **8**, 7(2), 48–52.

Grunwald, A. On reading and reading braille. Bethesda, Md: ERIC Document Reproduction Service, ED 015303, 1967.

Harris, A. and Sipay, E. *Effective teaching of reading.* New York: McKay, 1971.

Heber, R. A study of programmed instruction in braille. Bethesda, MD.: ERIC Document Reproduction Service, ED 015303, 1967.

Kederis, C. Training for increasing braille reading rates. Bethesda, MD.: ERIC Document Reproduction Service, ED 023229, 1971.

Mangold, S. The Mangold developmental program of tactile perception and braille letter recognition. Castro Valley, CA.: Exceptional Teaching Aids, 1977.

Mangold, S. The effects of a developmental teaching approach on tactile perception and braille letter recognition based on a model of precision teaching. San Francisco: California State University, 1977.

Mangold, S. The importance of precision teaching in the education of visually handicapped children. *Education of the Visually Handicapped,* Spring, 1978.

Mangold, S. Tactual perception and braille letter recognition: Effects of developmental teaching. *Journal of Visual Impairment and Blindness*, 72(7), 259-266.

McBride, V. Exploration of rapid reading in braille. *New Outlook for the Blind*, 1974, **68**, 8-13.

Olson, M. *The effects of training in rapid reading on the reading rate and comprehension of braille and large print readers.* Ann Arbor, MI: University Microfilms, 1975.

Spache, G. *The teaching of reading.* Bloomington, IN: Phi Delta Kappa, 1972.

Umsted, R. *Improvement of braille reading through code recognition and training.* Ann Arbor, MI: University Microfilms, 1970.

Umsted, R. Improving braille reading. *New Outlook for the Blind,* 1972, **66**, 169-177.

Wallace D. *The effect of rapid reading instruction and recognition training on the reading rate and comprehension of adult legally blind print and braille readers.* Unpublished doctoral dissertation, Brigham Young University, 1973.

Chapter V
Ideas for Working
with Problem Readers

A "problem reader" generally falls into one of two categories: He ha. either not learned to read in any other medium than braille, or is a former print reader. This does not imply that having once been a print reader makes a child a "problem brailler reader." If these students have difficulty with braille, they usually have had difficulty with print also. They will be considered a separate remedial group in this book, because their problems often need to be handled in a different way from those of children who have not been exposed to print.

Fourteen general areas of remediation will be first outlined and then discussed in this chapter. These remediation areas apply, no matter what the reader's background. Teachers may find that many students function high in all but one or two areas, and that altering their teaching approach is all that is needed. For example, a student who is poor in auditory discrimination and thus phonetic analysis, may not need "remediation" as such if the teacher presents her reading program by sight words and contextual reading.

After the discussion of general remedial areas, the factors unique to former print readers are presented.

General Areas of Remediation

For ease of discussion, the problems of remedial braille readers have been categorized into 14 general areas. For a more complete assessment checklist, see Appendix A, p. 99.

1) Book Handling/Posture
2) Locating Skills—book sections, page numbers, paragraphs, lines
3) Finger Curvature/Hand Relaxation
4) Lightness of Touch
5) Hand Movements—smoothness, continuity, independence
6) Symbol Recognition—letters, words, punctuation, numbers
7) Phonetic Analysis
8) Structural Analysis
9) Contextual Reading
10) Comprehension—literal, interpretative, critical/problem solving
11) Rate of Reading

12) Flexibility of Reading Rate—type of material, purpose for reading
13) Oral expression
14) Attitude/Motivation

Remediation Techniques

The remediation techniques discussed in this section are not comprehensive, but rather are intended as a few beginning guidelines. They may pertain to any problem reader, but teachers will need to tailor them to fit individual students and may expand upon them according to program resources. Many of the readiness or beginning reading activities suggested in Chapters Three and Four can be used with problem readers, though the focus of this section is on techniques that are an extension of such activities.

The appropriateness of any one technique will depend largely upon the student's previous reading program. In some cases, the student requiring remediation has learned from a single teacher, but more often than not, the student has been introduced to braille by someone other than the teacher providing remediation. It is therefore essential that a thorough assessment of each student's braille reading skills be completed before beginning any program of remediation.

Book Handling/Posture

The reader who tires quickly or is reading inefficiently because of awkward book handling must be given an opportunity to experiment with sitting postures and book position. The teacher might check the student's reading rate for each position he tries. If the student's body is tense, no reading posture will be efficient. It may be necessary to have the student lie on his back and listen to music in order to relax before beginning to read. A small vibrator used across the shoulder area also helps relieve muscle tension before braille reading. Once one or more postures have been identified as more comfortable and efficient, the student must commit himself to practice times throughout the day.

Locating Skills

The student who is unable to locate parts of a book or lines on a page may need to overlearn the basic concepts of top, bottom, right, left, beginning and end. [For a detailed discussion of how this may be accomplished, see the section on Concept Development in Chapter Three (pp. 26–29). The teacher may also make a time game of locating page numbers, paragraphs, and section headings. By disassembling old braille magazines, several worksheets can be prepared for the student to work on independently. The teacher directs the student to locate various items on a page by asking him to place push pins into the particle board to which the worksheet is attached. If the directions are put on tape, this activity can be carried out independently.

Finger Curvature / Hand Relaxation

For the student who is tracking braille with his fingers in a flat, out-stretched position, a book can be placed beneath each line of braille to force his fingers into a curved position. The thickness of the book should vary according to the length of the student's fingers from fingertip to knuckle.

If the student's hands seem tense or stiff, a warm-up relaxation period may be required at the beginning of each reading period. An exercise that is often helpful for relieving tension, as well as for strengthening muscles is palmer squeezing of rubber balls, clay or play doh. The student might also shake his fingers loosely in the air or roll objects with his palm against a table surface. If a student has cold hands, perhaps from poor circulation, a small hair dryer can be used for a quick "warm up."

Lightness of Touch

If a student's body is tense, he is likely to press too hard when reading braille. It is thus important to help the student relax his entire body. Tracking exercises for no comprehension may also prove necessary. If the teacher has not already used the activities suggested in Chapter Four, they may prove effective with the remedial braille reader.

Hand Movements

Students who scrub braille, backtrack over lines previously read, or use only one hand (when they have the potential to use two), will benefit from a program such as *The Mangold Developmental Program of Tactile Perception and Braille Letter Recognition*. As discussed in Chapter Four, part of this program is devoted to teaching smooth, continuous tracking patterns. Rate and performance criteria are built into carefully sequenced lessons. The teacher may also use language experience stories and memorized material to continue work on hand movements. Students are often surprised to find out that they pick up very little information during backtracking movements; regressive hand movements most often become merely inefficient habits. The teacher might begin to prove this to the student having him read two stories that are comparable in difficulty level and length. For one passage the student is then directed to read in any manner he chooses (backtracking included). The instructions for reading the second passage restrict the student to continuous reading with no backtracking allowed. By comparing the percent comprehension achieved on the two passages, the student should be able to see for himself the relative inefficiency of backtracking movements.

Symbol Recognition

If the student consistently makes errors in the decoding process he must first be observed to check how he positions his fingers with respect to the braille symbols. Braille characters are often misread because of inadequate fingertip coverage of the characters. The student may be missing dots and thus misinterpreting individual symbols. If the student's finger position is satisfactory, the teacher must next examine the type of decoding error being made.

If a student is confusing symbols which are reversible pairs [o/ow, e/i, r/w, m/sh, p/th, z/the, n/ed] or rotations of one another [s/wh, t/ou, h/j, ar/gh, ed/the, m/u, s/gh, er/with], one symbol of each pair needs to be overlearned before work begins on the other. Let us suppose that the student is confusing the letter *e* with the letter i. He should be given exercises which have e's mixed with other symbols in words and sentences. His only task would be to track the lines rapidly and verbally identify the e's. When this task is accomplished with 100 percent accuracy and at an approximate rate of 80 verbalized *e*'s per minute, the symbol is considered "overlearned." The next step in remediation would be to begin a similar drill on the symbol *i*. Once the *i* is also overlearned, the two symbols can be mixed in words and sentences for discrimination. It is also often helpful to give the student a "crutch" for remembering specific symbols. For example, in discriminating between the braille symbol for the number five and for the number nine, the crutch might be a saying: "The dots slant *up* for a nine because a nine is *higher* than a five." Additional ideas for overlearning symbol configurations can be found in Appendix C (pp. 106-107).

If the student is under ten years of age and making errors in identifying single letter contractions, a combination of brailled phonic exercises and cassette tape recordings is often effective. The American Printing House for the Blind has a series on braille code recognition that is recommended for students who are over ten years of age. *The Mangold Program of Tactile Perception and Braille Letter Recognition* is an additional resource for the teacher remediating braille letter recognition.

When the student leaves out words during oral reading, the teacher needs to check on the ensuing comprehension level. If leaving out words does not distort the meaning of the passage for the student, the teacher should not be concerned with remediating in this area. If, however, the meaning is altered, one technique to try involves the teacher reading to the student. As the student follows along on the braille line read by the teacher, he is asked to periodically fill in words whenever the teacher makes a deliberate pause.

Often a student consistently misses only particular words during oral reading. Should this happen, the teacher may again read aloud to the student at a rate close to the student's own reading rate. She should read the troublesome words more loudly than the other words on the page. Once the teacher has modelled this procedure several times, the student should take the teacher's role in reading aloud and emphasizing the troublesome words.

An additional exercise would be to provide the student with brailled worksheets. On some of the worksheets, sentences are written with troublesome words replaced by blanks. Other worksheets might consist of complete sentences containing the particular words the student is missing. On these exercises the student might be given points for each troublesome word he identifies. The teacher, on the other hand, would receive points for those remaining unidentified. If it seems suitable, the teacher may introduce time limits to the student's search using a kitchen timer or tape recording. The teacher will note that each of these exercises not only raises the student's level of awareness concerning the words he commonly misses, but also introduces extra drill on these words.

Phonetic Analysis

When a student is unable to decode words by phonetically breaking them down, the teacher must ask herself two basic questions. First, is the student able to hear the difference among various phonemes? Many students have basic auditory processing difficulties; decoding words by phonetic analysis is simply impractical for these students. Teachers must re-route their lessons to use some other approach for decoding words. The second question is: Does the student listen to the differences between sounds? In other words, does he require training in basic auditory discrimination or general listening skills? It is assumed that the student has had a recent hearing evaluation, so that a high frequency hearing loss can be ruled out. Individuals with high frequency hearing losses often do not hear certain phonemes; they are prone to "guess" at the sounds from the faulty auditory productions they have been receiving.

Once the teacher has established that a student has the ability to use phonetic analysis for decoding, she can proceed with specific remedial techniques for improving this skill. One of the methods that has been used successfully by many speech pathologists is that of kinesthetic-tactual sound reproduction. The student touches the teacher's throat and/or mouth while she is making a particular sound. The next step involves the student's attempting similar throat and mouth movements while producing the same sound. The teacher provides constant feedback to the child with repeated sessions of modelling. The student is asked to concentrate on the kinesthetic or internal feeling of sound production when he correctly approximates the sound. This approach is supplemented by the teacher's verbal explanations of how a particular sound is produced, e.g., tightness of vocal cords, amount of air explusion, position of the tongue.

Phonetic analysis often becomes easier for students when they use it in conjunction with contextual clues, word configuration, and structural analysis. Many basic phonic rules are learned incidentally in this manner.

Rhyming exercises have been used successfully by many teachers. Through these exercises the student may work on words that begin or end with the same consonant, words that contain the same short or long vowel sounds, words that contain the same blends, or words that contain the same digraphs. Blends and digraphs that form Grade 2 braille contractions should always be presented to the student in their contracted form, rather than in Grade 1 braille.

On occasion, a student is helped if a few basic phonic generalizations are drilled and memorized. One must not forget that phonetic analysis is a complex process. A single phoneme such as long "a" has eight possible sounds, depending upon what precedes and/or follows it (Bamman, Dawson, and McGovern, 1973). Clymer (1963) conducted a study on the utility of 45 commonly taught phonic generalizations. Using an arbitrary criterion of 75 percent utility, he determined that only 18 phonic generalizations were stated specifically enough to aid a student in pronunciation of words contained in the basic reading series that introduced the generalizations. The remaining 28 generalizations had too many exceptions to be useful 75 percent of the time. Below is the list of 18 that *did* meet his criterion:

1) The *r* gives the preceding vowel a sound that is neither long nor short.
2) Words having double *e* usually have the long *e* sound.
3) In *ay* the *y* is silent and gives *a* its long sound.
4) When y is the final letter in a word, it usually has a vowel sound.
5) When *c* and *h* are next to each other, they make only one sound.
6) *Ch* is usually pronounced as it is in *kitchen, catch,* and *chair,* not like *sh.*
7) When *c* is followed by *e* or *i*, the sound of *s* is likely to be heard.
8) When the letter *c* is followed by *o* or *a,* the sound of *k* is likely to be heard.
9) When *ght* is seen in a word, *gh* is silent.
10) When two of the same consonants are side by side only one is heard.
11) When a word ends in *ck*, it has the same last sound as in *look.*
12) In most two-syllable words, the first syllable is accented.
13) If *a, in, re, ex, de,* or *be* is the first syllable in a word, it is usually unaccented.
14) In most two-syllable words that end in a consonant followed by *y*, the first syllable is accented and the last is unaccented.
15) If the last syllable of a word ends in *le*, the consonant preceding the *le* usually begins the last syllable.
16) When the first vowel element in a word is followed by *th, ch,* or *sh,* these symbols are not broken when the word is divided into syllables and may go with either the first or second syllable.
17) When there is one *e* in a word that tends in a consonant, the *e* usually has a short sound.
18) When the last syllable is the sound *r*, it is unaccented.

If the teacher determines that a particular student might benefit from overlearning the above generalizations, she might braille them on individual index cards with examples. To further practice their use, these generalizations may be used in a game situation in which the student is asked to give an example of the phonic rule he has "spun" on a gameboard.

The regular classroom teacher may have any number of print games in her room for reinforcing phonic skills. The vision teacher may find that some of them are adaptable for use by braille students by simply transcribing print directions to braille and adding tactual objects to substitute for pictures. A few commercial games that are highly recommended are described below. The publisher's names and addresses can be found in Appendix D (pp. 108-109).

1) *Speech to Print Phonics*—This game is structured for group work through the use of pupil response cards. It includes work on auditory discrimination, letter names, letter sounds, letter combinations, and applications of these skills to word attack situations. In addition to stressing sounds, context and meaning receive attention.

2) *Phonics We Use Learning Games*—These games are attractive to children and require minimal teacher supervision. Included in this material are reinforcement exercises for learning the various consonant and vowel sounds and sound combinations.

3) *Consonant and Vowel Lotto*—These are two separate games which are most beneficial after the sounds have been taught.

Structural Analysis

Students having difficulty in the area of structural analysis of words usually find suffixes the most troublesome (Wilson, 1972). Compound words, though initially difficult to recognize, are easily broken into their component parts. When students still do not recognize the part, a sight word approach may be helpful. Because prefixes come at the beginning of words and have a definite effect on their meanings, they are easier to learn than suffixes. Most suffixes, when removed from their base words, leave these words with distorted configurations and spellings.

The teacher should consult any basal reading series for suggestions on remediating errors in structural analysis. Additionally, she might try the discovery approach to the study of specific prefixes, suffixes and compound words. Whenever these word parts form Grade 2 contractions, as in the example for teaching the prefix "dis" below, the teacher should present that word part in its contracted form.

1) Present a base word in a sentence. *I* **like** *school.*
2) Change the base word by adding the prefix. *I* **dislike** *school.*
3) Have the student generalize the difference in meaning between the first and second sentence.

4) Present several more words in similar manner: agree/disagree; appear/disappear; comfort/discomfort; connect/disconnect; honest/dishonest.

5) Help the student generalize by asking him what "dis" does to the meaning of a base word.

6) From a dictionary, examine several words that begin with "dis" and discuss with the student if they fit the generalization.

7) During contextual reading, continue to point out the prefix to the student. Again, reinforce its effect on base words.

Whenever the study of prefixes, suffices or compound words can be accomplished through games, the teacher must adapt such games for the braille student. Brailled game parts should then be interlined with manuscript print so that sighted classmates can read them. *The SRA Word Games Laboratory* has several well-developed games for reinforcement of instruction in structural analysis. They are generally interesting to the student and have the additional advantage of peer group learning.

Contextual Reading

Students who fail to use the relationship of words within phrases, sentences and paragraphs often have inadequate experiential backgrounds. Even if they were able to use contextual clues, they may not understand much of the vocabulary. When this is the case, the remedial teacher needs to alert the student's regular classroom teacher, his parents or primary caregivers. He will need to have as many "hands-on", direct experiences as possible.

Even when the student's experiential background is adequate, he may still not understand the function of context clues. Furthermore, when a student recognizes context clues once they are pointed out by the teacher, he may not able to anticipate them. Remediation of these difficulties requires a lot of direct instruction and practice on a variety of literary styles.

If a student makes an error on a word during oral reading, it is not wise for the teacher to stop and correct the student immediately. To do so, would prevent natural use of context. If the student reads to the end of a sentence and does not realize through distorted meaning that a mistake has been made, the teacher may then provide the correction.

One technique for teaching initial awareness of context clues is through forced-choice completion of blanks in sentences. Below is an example of the technique:

It was time for lunch. Dick had not eaten for many hours. He was very
_____.

1) happy   2) hungry   3) angry

A similar strategy involves the teacher's reading stories aloud to the student. These stories should be on topics of known interest to that individual. Occasionally the teacher pauses and leaves out critical words that the student can fill in by using context.

The Cloze Procedure, used to assess student reading level, can also be used for remediating context usage. The teacher types out a passage from a book that falls within the child's reading level. Blanks are placed at regular intervals (usually every fifth word) and the student is asked to fill them with words that fit. The words do not have to be exactly the same as the ones deleted by the teacher; so long as they mean approximately the same thing, the student is using context.

Sighted students have the advantage of pictures for picking up context clues from many stories. The vision teacher can substitute a tape recorded description for the braille student so that he, too, may learn to "read between the lines" through the use of pictorial description.

One last suggestion for remediating in this area is to provide students with ample opportunity to read materials of particular interest to them. Each day the student should be allowed some classroom time for "free reading."

Comprehension

Comprehension is perhaps the most complex of the skills involved in reading. Prior to discussing the specific types of comprehension, several general suggestions will be offered.

General Comprehension

The more an individual reads, the better he is likely to comprehend. One of the greatest problems in remediation, however, stems from the aversion most problem readers have to reading. How can a student be motivated to practice something at which he has experienced repeated failure? A crucial first step is for the teacher to discover what subjects the child enjoys. This may not be easy, since remedial students are not likely to express their interests to the teacher, even when they are specifically asked to do so. One way to obtain this information indirectly is through sentence completion exercises. The teacher reads statements such as those below and asks the students to fill in the blanks:

After school I like to _____.
When I have time to daydream, I imagine that I am _____.
If I could miss a week of school, I would _____.
My favorite TV program is _____.

Once the teacher has determined what the child's interests are, she should find easy reading material on those subjects.

A wide variety of reading materials must be available for the student to browse through and select for free reading time. The teacher might offer to read some books aloud, if they are beyond the student's reading level. Eventually the remedial student might be asked to contract with the teacher on the number of books he will read each week. When a book is selected initially, the teacher should help the student go through the book to pick out troublesome vocabulary words so that these can be explained ahead of time.

Even though the student may be having difficulty in comprehending what he reads, at least one-fourth of the remedial reading time should be spent allowing him to read silently. The amount of time spent in silent reading may be short initially but will increase gradually as the student improves. From time to time the teacher will need to check the student's comprehension in a non-threatening manner. Oftentimes, this is accomplished by asking questions related to the student's feelings or emotions.

Re-reading material is a helpful remedial technique in the area of comprehension; however, it can be a threatening experience if not carefully planned. Whenever possible, the student should be asked to read a passage silently the first time and orally with a classmate the second time.

Comprehension should not always be checked through questioning the student. Instead, the student might tape record his feelings, dramatize the story, or write a new ending for the story.

Literal Comprehension

Literal or factual comprehension often gets too much time in the regular classroom. Remembering the facts of a story should be emphasized as little as possible in the remedial setting.

It is important that braille readers learn to outline material for its factual content. The vision teacher should give the student several good models of outlines transcribed into braille. The outlines would ideally cover material the student has already read. Another method of teaching outlining skills is to have a student brainstorm everything he can think of about a hobby or favorite sport. He is then asked to sequence those facts so that they make sense to someone who is trying to learn about the hobby or sport. From the sequence a simple outline can be framed.

Motivating materials to use for teaching literal comprehension include dictionaries, cookbooks, and magazines. The teacher might also clip paragraphs out of stories in old braille magazines and ask the student to sequence them.

Interpretive Comprehension

When students are unable to interpret the meaning of a story, it is always possible that they have inappropriate backgrounds for going beyond the exact words on a page. It is the teacher's responsibility to ask questions concerning their general understanding of the subject before attempting to teach the skill of interpretation.

Initially, students should be given several examples of interpretations that have already been made on stories they have read. In this manner, it will be easier for them to understand what "reading between the lines" really means.

The teacher might paraphrase several paragraphs of a story and ask the student to match the paraphrased statement with the original paragraph. A matching exercise might also be done with topic sentences of paragraphs.

During the beginning stages of interpretive reading, it is important that the teacher probe for elaboration. This means that when the student begins to use his own words to describe what he has read, the teacher asks him questions or helps to express a partially formed idea.

Critical/Problem Solving Comprehension

To go beyond the meaning of the words on a page and to think creatively about content is the highest level of comprehension. Teachers must be very accepting of students' attempts at this process while constantly probing for more originality.

It is often motivating (and less threatening) to work on critical comprehension in small groups. The group brainstorms on questions such as: What would happen if the main character in this story had been a girl instead of a boy? Groups might also work on figures of speech such as "playing it cool." The task would be to guess at meanings. Asking students to make analogies is still another group activity that can help teach critical problem solving after reading.

Reading assignments for teaching critical problem solving must be kept highly interesting. After the student achieves some initial success, content materials that he may be reading in the regular classroom can be used for practicing this skill.

Role playing is also a useful activity for children who have difficulty reacting to creative reading. The records entitled *Teaching Reading Through Creative Movement* are recommended for making the transition from creative body actions to creative discussions of written material (see Appendix D, pp. 108-109).

Rate of Reading

If a student reads braille too slowly, he will not only be handicapped in keeping up with his print-reading peers, but will also become less motivated to read at all. Students read slowly for any number of reasons. Some students scrub vertically up and down the braille dots, others press down too heavily on them, while still others are character-by-character readers. In most cases, these slow readers had begun to memorize the braille code before they developed good mechanical tracking skills. The reader is referred to Chapter Four for ways of working on those mechanical skills.

Additional ideas for increasing braille reading rates will be discussed later in this chapter where the difficulties of former print readers are examined.

Flexibility of Reading Rate

Slow braille readers are also often "inflexible readers." That is, they read all material at the same time regardless of difficulty or purpose. Again, Chapter Four contains many good ideas for working on the flexibility of students' braille reading rates. Every idea is applicable to the remedial braille reader, though the difficulty level of materials used for practicing varying reading rates may have to be lower for the remedial reader. The contrast between types of reading materials may also need to be accentuated. Open book evaluations are good for helping cautious readers to scan reading material for specific information. Initially, the student should not be given time limits on these evaluation. Later, however, timing and charting reading rates on both skimming and scanning activities will be essential.

Oral Expression

Braille students who use poor expression during reading aloud can often be helped through reading aloud in groups (choral reading). Another worthwhile remedial technique is to tape motivating stories for students to listen to during free time. When students write their own language experience stories, they are often able to practice good oral expression more naturally. When the student begins to make progress on his own oral expression, the teacher might introduce the "distortion game." In this game the teacher reads a story aloud to the student, but deliberately distorts its meaning through innapropriate oral expression. The student is then asked to identify the teacher's mistakes and to correct them.

Attitude/Motivation

Attitude and motivation were covered quite extensively in Chapters Three and Four. The reader is also referred to the final section of the present chapter for further suggestions for working with former print readers. Perhaps the most important thing to remember when trying to remediate in this area is pacing. Students who have built up negative feelings about reading must not be rushed into reading of any kind. There must be time for desensitization to the act of reading. This may mean that teacher and student spend time talking, walking, and discussing interesting subjects. When the teacher senses that the student is sufficiently relaxed, she might have the student dictate a story based on a recent personal experience he had. Initially any reading activity should be performed only by the teacher. Beyond experience stories, materials such as comic books, adventure stories, recipes or toy assembly directions might be transcribed for use.

The student might also listen to a tape simultaneously with reading these braille materials.

Working with Former Print Readers

If students have had difficulty with reading print, they probably will also have difficulty with braille. Many of the remediation techniques previously discussed in this chapter will be appropriate for these former print readers. On the other hand, there are some unique factors a teacher must consider when doing remedial work with these students. It is the purpose of this section to discuss those factors and to suggest ways to deal with them.

Motivation

The former print reader most often has a large psychological hurdle to overcome with respect to his loss of sight. Forcing braille instruction on him before he is psychologically "ready" is both unwise and wasteful of time. A sensitive parent or teacher must ascertain how well the child is progressing with respect to accepting his visual loss. When print can no longer be read with maximum magnification or becomes too fatiguing, braille may be considered. At this point it is important to ask the child what he knows about braille and how he feels about it. If a braille-reading child of the same age can be located, it is good to arrange for an informal meeting between them. It is ideal if this braille reading student also once read print, though this kind of match may be difficult to find. If regular tutoring by such a fellow student can be arranged, this may also serve to motivate the former print reader to approach braille more positively.

The teacher can heighten the student's interest in braille if she helps him make braille labels for this personal belongings. She might also braille material the student has memorized or written to let him examine on his own.

Tracking

The mechanics of tracking with the hands will be totally foreign to the former print reader. The use of simulated materials and repetitious braille discussed in Chapter Four would be very appropriate for this student, just as it is appropriate for the young child who has not read in a medium other than braille. Precision teaching with the use of rate and accuracy goals can be very helpful for reassuring the student that he is making progress. A readiness program such as the *Mangold Developmental Program of Tactile Perception and Braille Letter Recognition* provides the teacher with ready-made performance criteria on these mechanical skills. As was emphasized in Chapter Four, mechanical skills need to be well developed before the student is asked to work on discrimination of the braille characters.

Tactile Perception

It will not be necessary to go back as far in this area with the former print reader as it would be for the young beginning braille reader. While a short time may be spent detecting gradations of sandpaper or types of fabric, the teacher will want to move rapidly into discrimination of the braille cell. Flashcards and card games are motivating means of drilling letter or word recognition. Whenever possible, flash cards should contain the letter or word in context as well as in isolation. Again, the *Mangold Program* is a helpful set of materials for teaching letter recognition.

If there has been no history of difficulty in reading print, and most of the letters have been learned, the student should be started on some high interest low vocabulary materials. Below is a list of companies that publish materials of this nature. [See Appendix D (p. 109) for the address of each publisher.]

Benefit Press - Series on cowboys, space science, mystery adventure, trucks, animals, helicopters, racing are available with reading levels as low as pre-primer and interest levels as high as grade twelve.

Child's World Company - Series on sports superstars and rock and pop stars are published with reading levels down to third grade and interest levels as high as grade twelve.

Frank E. Richards Publishing Company - This company has re-written many of the classics in shortened versions with easier vocabulary words and less complex sentence structures.

Paperback Book Supply Company - Series on sports superstars, super-bowl champions, rock and roll stars and movie/t.v. entertainers are available with reading levels around grade six and interest levels as high as grade twelve.

Speed Building

It is very important that the former print reader does not become a "scrubber" or an analytical reader. "Scrubbing" is defined here as moving the fingertips up and down over the braille cells as opposed to a smooth horizontal sweeping across them. An analytical reader may become a "scrubber" as he attempts to get meaning from each cell rather than from words or word combinations. If his rate is too slow, the print images of letters are often recalled visually as he comes in contact with the corresponding braille symbols. This "intermediate" association is not good, because it will prevent efficient reading in the long term. There are several techniques for building speed with former print readers. Many of these, of course, are useful to all readers.

Warm-Up Tracking

A minimum of ten minutes should be devoted to warm-up tracking at the beginning of each reading period. This calls for hand movements across and down a page at a rate that allows for no symbol recognition. This can also be a time for the student to practice independent hand movements and new patterns of tracking down a page. Each day the student should strive to cover more pages in a specified period of time while still attempting no symbol recognition.

A good way to work gradually into reading for comprehension is to have the student do some "bits and pieces" reading. This type of reading was described in Chapter Four under the topic of scanning and skimming. The student locates one or two words on a braille page by random pointing. He then tracks at a rapid pace down the page in an attempt to relocate those word(s). From these initial words, the student can be asked to find more words in the same way until he has the "thread of the story" on that page. After several re-readings, the student's rate should not have decreased significantly, while smooth, rapid movements should be feeling more natural to him by this time.

An additional warm-up exercise a student might do is repeated tracking over a familiar sentence or passage. Each re-reading should be done at a faster rate than the previous time. This type of practice encourages the student to read in "chunks" as well as to make rapid judgments about the tactual configuration of a word based on its beginning structure and its use in context.

Low Level Material

Material used for speed building ought to be at least three to four grade levels below the student's independent reading level. This material should be as high in interest as possible. Although some high interest low vocabulary books that are commercially available will be suitable, it might also be advantageous for the teacher to braille some original passages based upon the student's interest and hobbies.

Flashcards of Common Words

Flashcards with the most commonly occurring words should be brailled for the student. Among these words should also be the "sign-post" and "turn-about" words described in Chapter Four. A non-slip reading pad should be provided for use with flashcards. As previously mentioned, flashcards should have a phrase or sentence that uses the word in context as well as presenting it in isolation. Again, some identification of "top" and "bottom" is necessary. This can be achieved by clipping off one corner of the card or simply notching the top of the card.

Braille With Tape

When the student has begun reading in a regular reading series, some of the stories should be taped for him. He can then listen to the tape as he tracks across the corresponding braille. When he is able to keep up with the normal speaking rate on the tape, a compressed speech device might be used to increase the speaking rate even further. Again, this forces the braille reader to make rapid associations between the moving tactual con-figurations and their meanings in context.

Goal Setting / Timing / Charting

At each reading period, the student's reading rate should be measured. A goal for the period's end and the next day's session should be set. Tim-ings can be accomplished independently by the student if the teacher records several time intervals on tape with the words "start" and "stop". The timings should start at thirty seconds and one minute, gradually building up to five minutes. The student needs encouragement to record his daily progress and perhaps to construct a tactual graph of this progress over time.

Blocking Subvocalizations

When a student is first learning braille there will be a great temptation to subvocalize words he is reading. Subvocalization not only slows reading rate but also allows the student time to visualize print symbols as an in-termediate step between tactual contact and brain interpretation. In addi-tion to the warm-up exercises previously suggested, the teacher can try two additional interventions. By having the student place a pencil between his teeth, he has a constant reminder not to move his mouth in subvocaliza-tion. Gum chewing is another technique that has worked. For short reading periods it also has a "pacing" effect. An over-working of the jaw over a long period may, however, destroy the effect.

References

Bammen, H., Dawson, M. and McGovern, J. *Fundamentals of basic reading in-struction.* New York: David McKay, 1973.

Clymer, T. The utility of phonic generalizations in the primary grades. *The Reading Teacher*, 1963, **16**(4), 252-258.

Harris, A. and Sipay, E. *Effective teaching of reading.* New York: David McKay, 1971.

Herr, S. *Learning activities for reading.* Dubuque, Iowa: Wm. C. Brown, 1970.

Spache, G. *The teaching of reading.* Bloomington, Indiana: Phi Delta Kappa, 1972.

Wilson, R. *Diagnosis and remedial reading for classroom and clinic.* Columbus, Ohio: Charles E. Merrill, 1972.

Chapter VI
Adding Spice to a
Braille Reading Program with
Activities and Games

By Sally S. Mangold, Ph.D.
Associate Professor of Special Education
San Francisco State University

It is impossible to overemphasize the importance of helping children to become efficient readers. The ability to read skillfully is becoming increasingly important in every aspect of modern living. It is the responsibility of the schools to provide a well balanced program which is designed to help children develop the needed skills that are essential in everyday life.

A well balanced reading program includes a variety of reading experiences—developmental, functional, and recreational. Each makes a significant contribution to the child's learning: A developmental program provides systematic instruction in reading skills; a functional program is concerned with the use of reading skills to accomplish a specific purpose, such as reading to locate information; recreational reading develops desirable reading interests and stimulates each child to read widely for pleasure, both through books and games.

This chapter is limited to the use of activities and games as they relate to the recreational aspects of a good reading program. Games are a fun way to provide repeated exposure to appropriate vocabulary, while maintaining a high level of motivation for learning to read. The activities and games suggested in this chapter will be described for their appropriateness to numerous skill areas.

Reading Readiness

Reading readiness is a state of general maturity which allows a child to learn to read with understanding and without difficulty. A multi-media, multi-sensory approach is the most effective at this level. Braille users should be encouraged to use all of their residual vision to explore their environment and complete activities. Following is an outline of the readiness skills that need to be mastered by pre-braille students. These skills may easily be turned into games by giving points to the student for each correct response and giving the teacher a point for each incorrect response. (Activities should be adjusted so that the student wins most of the time.)

Determining Likes and Differences
Sorting Objects
1. By texture—soft, rough, hard, smooth
2. By physical properties—round, square, thick, thin
3. By function—things that belong in the bathroom, things that are found in the kitchen, things you would find in the yard, things you use when you eat
4. By size—things that will fit in your pocket, things that will fit in the little bottle and the big bottle
5. By size—things like nuts: brazil nuts, walnuts, peanuts

Determining Whether Objects Are the Same or Different
When students are asked to compare two objects, be certain that the questions are specific. An example follows: Teacher gives student a knife and fork.

Teacher: "Are these two objects the same?"
Student: "Yes".
Teacher: "No they are different, because they are different lengths, etc. Note: The student may have said "Yes" because he recognized that both the knife and fork were of metal.

Be certain to always have the student verbalize the characteristics that make two things either the same or different.
1. Same or different by texture
2. Same or different by function
3. Same or different by size

Identify the One Object Which is Different in a Large Group of Objects
1. A peanut mixed in with 10 or 12 walnuts
2. A spoon mixed in with a number of forks
3. A straw mixed in with a number of pencils

Identify the One Object Which is Different From Two Like Objects
1. By texture
2. By function
3. By size
4. By color (when possible)

Developing Meaningful Language
1. Ask the children to bring to school toys, souvenirs, collections or favorite possessions, which might be shared with the group.
   The teacher asks each child to show some object and then to tell all about it. After the students understand this activity, ask them all to bring the same type of object on the same day. (A hat your father wears when he is working; a beautiful leaf; a favorite stuffed animal.)

At this age sighted students are beginning to detect subtle differences between similar objects. When you provide a visually handicapped student with an opportunity to compare a number of objects from the same category, you have reduced his environment to a manageable size.

The teacher keeps lists of appropriate descriptive words and uses as many as possible when the visually handicapped student is examining different objects. This is the only means of building a meaningful vocabulary.

2. The teacher reads a story to the children, then asks the children to create a new ending for the story.
3. Present the class with an unusual object they would not recognize. Ask them to make up a story to tell for what purpose the object could be used.
4. Have the children make hand puppets with styrofoam balls, sticks for handles, buttons for eyes, fabric for ears, which are pinned on with straight pins. Ask the children to make up a story about their puppet and where he likes to go.
5. Game—Mr. and Mrs. Potato Head—for identifying parts of the body; available in department or toy stores.
6. Dramatic play—using hand puppets, have the children act out members of the family.
7. *Word by Word Circle Game*—The children sit in a circle. The teacher or child starts off with a word, such as "George." The next child adds another word repeating the first, "George was," each child adds a new word until a complete sentence has been spoken. The game may be continued until a complete story has been told about George.
8. Creating Endings—A three or four line story which is unknown to the children is read. The children create an ending for the story.

   Danny and Rick went for a walk in the woods. When they were deep in the woods they heard a strange sound. They looked back and saw..."
9. Rhyming Game—The teacher shows the children hand or finger puppets.
   Teacher: "Each little rhyme will end with a word that rhymes with the names of the puppet."
   (e.g. This little boy is Bill. Bill lives on a _____. This little girl is Sue. Sue's favorite color is _____.)
10. Crazy Rhymes—See the cat wearing a hat,
    The big bad goat ate my _____.

Developing Motor Control

A. *Dramatic Plays*—The teacher reads a story such as "Three Billy Goats Gruff" and the children act out the story.

B. Creating a whole:

1. Construction blocks
2. Simple shape puzzles
3. Use of tools (saw, hammer, nails)
4. Peg board
5. Nesting toys
6. Poppet beads

C. Use of outdoor play equipment

D. Coloring—Make raised line shapes by using tracing wheel on the reverse side of braille paper. The paper is placed on top of a thin piece of cardboard. The desired shape is then pressed with the tracing wheel. Students may be asked to color inside of the raised shapes. A raised line braille coloring book, *Touch and Color* is available from ETA (see p. 111).

E. Cutting with scissors—always use very sharp sewing scissors when the child is cutting under supervision. Be sure to use blunt nosed scissors when the child is working independently.

1. Give child a piece of heavy construction paper 1½" wide. Teach the student to cut all the way across and continue cutting until the strip of paper has been cut into many, many tiny pieces. These pieces of paper may be glued down to make a collage.
2. Give the child a strip of construction paper 2" wide. Teach the child to cut almost all the way across. Continue making cuts across the strip of paper until he reaches the opposite end. Teach the child to roll the cut sections around a pencil to make the sections curl. The

two ends may be stapled together to make a headband.
3. Give the student a large piece of construction paper. Have him make cuts all the way around the perimeter of the paper. This could be used as a place mat for a party, or as a decoration on a display table.
4. Cut a desired shape out of cardboard (keep it simple). Staple the cardboard shape on top of medium weight construction paper. Teach the student to follow the cut cardboard when using his scissors. After he has cut out a shape by following the shape of the stapled cardboard, remove the cardboard.

F. Folding and Tearing Paper—Shapes may be made on construction paper using a tracing wheel, which has rather large teeth. The student may be taught to tear along this line in order to make the shape that has been drawn.

G. Rhythms
1. Hopping, skipping, and running to music
2. Dancing
3. a. Creative   b. Repeating a pattern that has been taught
   c. Dancing with a partner

H. Bouncing a Large Rubber Ball
1. Up and down to yourself   2. Back and forth to another person

I. Throwing sandbags—An audible target helps focus the direction of the throw. A large board may be made which contains a number of different sized holes, a radio may be placed back of the board to indicate to the child the direction of the target. For children who have difficulty, use a large box which is placed so that the open side faces the child. Place a radio back of the box to provide an audible indication of the direction of the box.

J. Walking a Balancing Beam
1. Broadside   2. Narrowside

Developing Left or Right Directionality

Pegboard—use two pegboards. Use the first board to set up the activity in its final completed form. Teach the student to examine your model by always beginning at the left side and going across each line. This allows the student to work independently when you are not available. He may keep checking your model to remind him of the desired finished product, and he may also use your model to check his work when the task is completed.

1. Place one peg in each hole beginning at the left side of each line and go all the way across the board.
2. Place one peg in *every other* hole on each line beginning at the left and going across the board.
3. Place a peg in the first hole and the last hole of each line.
4. Place one peg in the first line, two pegs in the second, three pegs in the third line, etc.

The Magnet and Square Game

Using a Stokes Placeholder [available from American Printing House for the Blind (APH)], place raised line graph paper [available from APH] on the top of the metal board. Direct the student to place a small magnet in each of the squares. Always begin at the left margin and go across the page. When the teacher says "GO" the student begins to put one magnet in each square. After 60 seconds the teacher says "STOP." The student gets one point for each square that contains a magnet. The teacher gets one point for each square that does not contain a magnet. The one with the most points wins the game.

Variation: Have the student put one fuzzy pregummed circle inside each square. (Fuzzy circles available at most stationery stores.)

Raised Line Game

Teacher rolls a sheet of raised line paper [available from APH] into a braille writer. A full braille cell is placed at the left end, and right end of each line. The paper is then removed from the braille writer and placed on the table in front of the student. The student is directed to take a crayon, begin at the left end of the line and follow the raised line all the way across the page until he touches the full cell at the right side of the page. One point is given for each line that is correctly followed.

Note: Many activities for left to right sequencing are presented in the *Mangold Developmental Program of Tactual Perception and Braille Letter Recognition. (Exceptional Teaching Aids, 20102 Woodbine Avenue, Castro Valley, California 94546.)*

Tactual Perception

A. Fabric Dominoes

B. Dot Dominoes Patterns of pregummed fuzzy dots are placed on heavy tag board to make large dominoes. (The fabric or the dot dominoes should be used on a nonslip surface, i.e., is either rubber or flannel covered.)

Identifying Similar Shapes

The teacher cuts heavy cardboard into shapes (circle, square, triangle, rectangle). The student sorts the shapes and puts them in the appropriate slot which has been cut in the top of a shoe box.

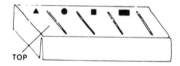

Tape appropriate shape next to slot. If box is covered with contact paper, taped down shapes may be easily changed for new activities.

Variation: The same shape may be used in four different sizes.
Variation: The same shapes may be used in four different textures.

Bridging the Gap Between Real Objects and Formal Braille Reading

Children who demonstrate the ability to discriminate tactually between real objects in their environment, between textures of like objects, and among subtle differences in size and shape of real objects, are ready to begin developing tactual perception skills necessary for mastery of braille. Fourteen carefully sequenced lessons, including many games, can be found in the *Mangold Developmental Program of Tactual Perception and Braille Letter Recognition*. For a more complete description of this program, see Chapter Four.

Developing Auditory Discrimination and Memory

Sounds Around Us
1. Take a walk. Stop and ask the student to listen. Ask the student to dictate a list of things that he heard during the one minute he was listening. Take another walk on another day. Read to the student the list of things that he heard on the first day. See how many new sounds he can identify on the second walk.
2. Listen to a tape recording or records that contain familiar sounds, telephone, alarm clock, water running, food frying, etc., (many commercial record companies have produced sound records and tapes). Practice identifying the familiar sounds.
3. Tap different surfaces that are in the classroom and help the student identify the material from which the objects were made.
   Teacher: Tap two or three things in sequence, the student then tries to identify the objects that were tapped and place them in the order in which they were tapped.
4. *The Tapping Game*
   The teacher selects two objects in the room, one object she taps very loudly; one she taps very softly. The student is asked to identify the loud sound, then to identify the soft sound. This game may continue until the teacher is tapping two things softly and two things loudly, etc.

Sound Blocks
1. Practice in the discrimination of sound may be provided by asking students to discriminate between high and low sound blocks that have been struck with a mallet. High/low are the easiest to discriminate.
2. Teacher makes a series of high/low sounds and ask the student to repeat the same rhythm saying "High/low."
   Example: High high high, low low low, high high, low low, high low high, high low high.
3. Give the student a number of individual sound blocks and ask him to place them in sequence with the lowest sound on the left and the highest sound on the right.

Clock and Watch Games
Place a loud ticking alarm clock somewhere in the classroom. Set a timer for five minutes and instruct the student to locate the ticking clock. If he finds the clock within five minutes he wins the game. After the student can locate the loud ticking clock easily, substitute a loud ticking pocket watch.

Follow the Leader
Ask the student to imitate everything you are doing—opening doors, opening drawers, placing a book on the table, pushing a chair under a table, getting a drink of water.

Guess Who I Am
Students line up behind one chair. The child sitting in the chair covers his eyes (when appropriate). The first child standing back of the chair says, "Guess who I am." If the student in the chair guesses correctly he may have another turn. If he misses, he must go to the end of the line.

Note: This game helps sighted students in a regular classroom to understand how difficult it sometimes is to recognize people by their voices.

Listening for Detail
Tell a short story. Ask the student such questions as:

1. What did Jimmy do first when he arrived at the party?
2. What was Jimmy's favorite toy?
3. How long did Jimmy's mother want him to stay at the park?
   Teacher: What does the ball do when it is dropped?
   "Bounce."
   What does the angry dog say?
   "Bow-wow."

After the children understand the game, a student who says a right answer may make up a question for another student. A number of students may be divided into two teams. One point is given to each team when a member of that team gives a correct answer.

Teaching Pre-Primer Concepts
It is vital for a student to understand the concepts that will be presented in the pre-primers. The sighted student obtains many clues about various experiences by looking at the pictorial representations in the reader. A blind student, on the other hand, must have experienced the activities himself if he is to benefit from the discussion that will be carried out in the reading circle.

A list of concepts presented in a pre-primer may be compiled and given to the student's parents, so that everyone in the student's learning environment may contribute activities and games that will strengthen the student's understanding of the world in which he lives. Typical pre-primer activities are riding a pony, going to the park, riding in an airplane, using an umbrella when it rains, helping mother cook in the kitchen, and going to the store to buy new shoes.

Regular classroom teachers frequently make large wall charts that contain pictures of all the characters who will be met in the pre-primer story.

Small dolls may be provided for the braille user. If the printed names are placed on the wall chart next to the pictures, be certain that a braille label is made for each of the dolls, so that the student may become very familiar with the configuration of each character's name.

Launching a Formal Reading Program in the Primary Grades

Charts: Various kinds of charts are widely used in the primary grades. Holding and manipulating a book is postponed so that the child is confronted with only one mechanical task of reading at a time.

Experience Charts
The content of the charts should reflect the child's experiences. The acquisition of good reading skills is greatly enhanced if the child quickly sees the relationship between the abstract symbols and the real world around him.

Pictures and drawings that illustrate the content of charts reinforce this concept for sighted students. Whenever possible, provide a real object for the braille user to remind him of the content of the chart.

Examples:

Page 1

I like Gum.
Gum is good.

Glue down a piece of GUM.

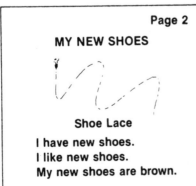

Page 2

MY NEW SHOES

Shoe Lace

I have new shoes.
I like new shoes.
My new shoes are brown.

Glue down a real shoelace

After the page is brailled, the inkprint should be placed *above* the braille so that the regular teacher can read the copy without disturbing the position of the child's hands.

Example: Note—The teacher brings a bird in a cage to show to the students.

Page 4

Glue down real feather.

Henry is a bird.
Henry is soft.
I like Henry.
Henry lives in a cage.

Word and Phrase Charts

Many classroom teachers write new vocabulary and phrases on separate strips of heavy tag board. The strips are pinned on bulletin boards or placed in pocket charts, as they are introduced. A duplicate set of braille strips are to be provided for the braille user. The interlining (print above the braille) should be done in felt tip pen in manuscript form so that other primary sighted children, who only read manuscript, can participate in many games with braille users. A textured rubber pad or felt covered board should be placed on the reading surface so that the braille cards do not slip easily.

Enrichment Charts

1. Calendar
2. Rules of the school
3. Menus
4. Names and duties of monitors
5. List of birthdays

Note: Everything that is found in regular chart form in a classroom should be brailled and made available to the braille user. Many teachers like to bind the stories or charts together into a small booklet or place them in pockets along the perimeter of a room, at a level that can be reached by a braille user.

Braille Letter Recognition

The Mangold Developmental Program of Tactual Perception and Braille Letter Recognition. See Chapter Four.

Braille letters are introduced in the Mangold Reading Program after the student has mastered 14 skills of Tactual Perception. Beginning on page 106 exercises that introduce one letter at a time are provided. No reversible pairs are ever introduced simultaneously. The following games from the Mangold Reading Program may be used to reinforce letter recognition.

Braille
Page 111

LETTER GAME. . .Cut out the playing cards. Tape them to heavy paper so that they do not bend easily.

Place the deck of cards with the braille side upwards in a small box on the middle of the table. Each student in turn takes one card off the top of the deck. He must read the braille letter in the upper left-hand corner. If he reads the card correctly, he may put that card in front of him on the table. If he does not read it correctly, he must give it to the other player. When all the cards are gone from the deck, the player with the most cards wins the game.

111

C	C	C
ɔ	ɔ	ɔ
g	g	g
მ	მ	მ
1	1	1
⌐	⌐	⌐

84

Braille   **RACING GAME.**
Page 121   Two players sit across the table from one another. Both players
locate the thick line in the middle of the page. Both players put
a magnet in the square that contains the letter (c) in the row
nearest to the thick line (upper left square). The player takes
turns rolling the die. They move their magnet from left to right
according to the number on the die. If they can read the letter
in the square on which they land, they may stay there. If they
cannot read the letter they must go back to the beginning. The
first player to move acorss all of the squares from left to right
wins the game.

121

p	ʌ	ɓ	ɔ	l
ʌ	p	l	ɓ	ɔ

- -
- -

c	g	l	d	y
l	c	g	y	d

Braille
Page 135

THE WIGGLE WORM GAME

The page should be placed upon the table so that the three holes are nearest to the player. Each player will begin the game with his magnet in the space to the right of the worm's head. He will continue moving his magnet until he reaches the tail of the worm. The first player to reach the tail, wins the game.

The number of spaces that each player may move will be indicated by the roll of the die. If the player can read the name of the letter on that space he may stay there. If he cannot read the name of the letter he must go back to the beginning space again.

135

86

Braille Cut out and prepare these playing cards as in Lesson 15.
Page 142 Use for the card game, "CONCENTRATION".

CONCENTRATION
Lay all the cards face down on the table. Each player in turn picks out two cards. If they do not make a match they must be returned to the same space on the table. Each player does this in turn until all the cards have been used up. Who ever has the most pairs in his possession wins the game.

		142
g	g	c
б	б	ɔ
c	l	l
ɔ	l	l
d	d	y
p	p	ʎ

Braille
Page 159

EGG CARTON GAME.
The letters in the top two lines should be cut out and attached to the bottom of each cup in an egg carton. Use double sided transparent tape for attaching the letters. The bottom two lines of letters may be used to prepare a second egg carton. Tape or staple the two egg cartons end to end, with all of the letters pointing in the same direction. Both players sit on the same side of the table. One player will move his marker across the top row and the other player will move his marker across the bottom row. Pingpong balls may be used for markers. The roll of the die indicates how far each player may move. the player must read correctly the letter in the cup where the marker lands. If he does not read it correctly, he must move his marker back three spaces or to the first cup if there are not three spaces. The first player to reach the opposite end of the two cartons wins the game.

159

g	c	l	d	y	a
b	s	w	p	o	k
g	c	l	d	y	a
b	s	w	p	o	k

Braille   Have the student decorate this face by adding materials for
Page 166   eyes, nose, hair, etc. Put a slit for a mouth on the line in-
             dicated.

Braille
Page 167

Cut out these tongues and use them with the face on the previous page. Put them through the slit from the back side so that the student may read the letters as they come out of the mouth. Attach the tongues to heavier paper if they seem too difficult to handle.

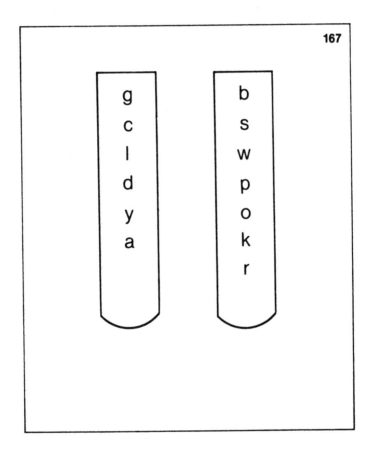

167

g
c
l
d
y
a

b
s
w
p
o
k
r

Braille
Page 190
and 191

These pages are identical.

QUICK ANSWER GAME.

Each of the two players places a game sheet on the magnet board. The first locates the upper left square which contains an (x). The die is rolled, the player counts the number of squares indicated by the die. He must locate the correct square and say aloud the correct letter in that square before the other players count to five. If he says it correctly he may move his magnet to that square. If he does not say it correctly he must move his magnet back to square one. The first person to move his magnet across all three lines of squares and lands on the bottom right square (which contains a d) wins the game.

190

x	g	n	c	l	h
d	e	y	m	a	r
b	k	s	o	w	d

Letter Bingo—Each player has a card marked off into 25 squares (the large raised line graph paper from APH may be used). In each square a letter is placed. A small number of individual cards containing one letter each are brailled. The upper right hand corner maybe cut or the top edge maybe pinked so that the student will place the card correctly in front of him. The teacher shows a single letter card to the student. The student reads his large letter bingo card, and if he locates an identical letter he places a magnet on that letter. When each letter in a row has been marked with a magnet, the student says "Bingo."

Self Correcting Letter Game
The teacher makes a series of small pages and binds them together as a book. Each of the 4 lines on the page contains a number and a letter.

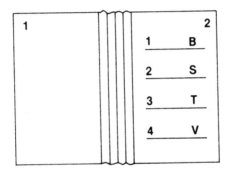

Note: (tape or record) (Which number is followed by a letter that sounds like the first sound you hear in 'sun'?) Leave blank spaces...student stops recorder, selects answer, then listens for answer on tape. Answer: 2

The Shoe-Box Letter Game
Using the same shoe-box that was made earlier for sorting shapes, attach a letter next to each slot in the top of the box. Have a student sort the letters and put them in the appropriate slots. One point is given for each correctly sorted letter. The teacher gets one point for each card that is incorrectly sorted. The one with the most points wins the game.

Treasure Box
The teacher places the box full of objects before the student. Brailled letter cards are taped to the bottom of each cup in a large muffin tin. When the teacher says "GO" the students removes an object and finds the muffin tin that represents the beginning sound of each object. He then places the object in the correct tin. One point is given for each correctly placed object.

Word Recognition

Initial consonant sounds in words. Mark the words that begin with the same sound as the object on top of the page.

Example:

•	GUM **4**
•	go, see, get, mother,
	ball, ride,
•	goat, coat

Page 4

Words That Start the Same

Mark the word that begins like the first word in each line.

Example: Jump, run, play, Judy
               Ball, coat, ride, big
               Mother, tip, go, my, see

Fishing for Words

Word cards are brailled, folded, and the open ends are pinned together with a large straight pin. Be sure to use steel pins, or hair pins, because a magnet will not pick up ordinary pins. The pinned cards are placed in a large fish bowl. The child lowers a piece of string with a small magnet attached to the string, into the fish bowl, and pulls out a 'fish.' If the child can read the card correctly he may keep it. If he cannot read the card correctly, the discarded card goes into another fish bowl to be used at a later time. (The fish that are caught may be strung on a piece of fishing line and hung by a pin from the bulletin board.) Each day the child reads the "fish" that he caught the day before, and then tries to catch other fish that are left in the bowl.

Words Category Game

Flash cards are made using the student's reading vocabulary. (The upper right corner may be clipped, so that the student will identify the top edge of the card when it is placed correctly on the rubber pad in front of him.) Three milk cartons are taped together and placed at the top of the rubber pad. The student is told by the teacher that each card belongs in a category and that the student should place the card in the correct box. Example:

1. Things people can do—see, ride, go, jump, sleep.
2. Names of people—Mother, Father, Sue, Tim
3. Names of things—car, skate, house, box, ball

The student is given one point for each correct response.

Treasure House Game
(This game may be played after the student has mastered initial and final consonant sounds and short vowel sounds.) The student is given a small wooden chest full of familiar objects. A treasure house (18″ x 18″ box which has dividers placed inside). Short vowel sounding words are brailled and taped to the bottom of each square. The student is directed to select an object from the treasure chest and place it where it belongs in the treasure house. A point is given for each correctly placed object.

hat	cap	rag	pin	fan	bell	gum	pan	pill

Wheel of Fortune
A large circle is cut out of cardboard. The vocabulary words from the student's reader are brailled and taped around the edge of the circle. The circle is attached to a permanent piece of cardboard by a loose-fitting brad placed in the center. A large cut arrow points from the bottom of the permanent cardboard up to the center of the circle at the bottom. The wheel is spun and when it stops the student is asked to read the word just above the tip of the arrow. The student is given one point for each word read correctly.

Word Families
Introduce the notion of word families.
AME family - game same came name
ILL family - pill Phil Bill hill
Attach a family name to each pocket in a notebook, containing a series of pockets.

```
 •
         page of
 •       note book
         _____

 •       pocket
```

Example: *Lost Children Game*
Appoint one student to be Police Captain. The other children are policemen. The teacher tells the police captain that she is Mrs. Ame. She has lost her children while on a picnic in the park. The police captain then tells the policemen to hunt for the lost children. Some of the policemen might look through a box marked "Playground," another through a box marked "Missing Persons"; another through a box marked "Ice-Cream Shop." When they locate the missing children, they remove

the area in which they were found and then place them in the correct pocket in the pocket note book.

Labeling

It is impossible to provide the braille user with the quantity of exposure to written form that is provided the sighted child, so we must avail ourselves of every opportunity to use daily experiences: (a) When the children bring in toys these may be labeled; (b) Areas in the classroom may be labeled—shelves and their purpose, fun books to read, math books, science books, etc., (c) Drawers according to content, scissors, paper, pencils, crayons, records, etc.

Labeling at home helps the braille user begin to organize his environment at home and in the classroom. Mother may have basic canned goods that she buys frequently, if so, encourage her to put braille labels on the appropriate shelf areas, e.g., peas, corn, beans, tuna. When she brings food home from the store have her ask the blind student to help her put away her canned goods. Some parents used canned labeling kits available from the American Foundation for the Blind, and attach labels to each of the canned goods. Other frequently used areas in the home may be labeled. Favorite records may be labeled, and tools in the garage may be identified by labels.

Sentence Recognition

Individualized Stories - Each student may dictate his own story to the teacher. The teacher simplifies the vocabulary so that it is appropriate for the child to read. The child may then read this story to another classmate or record it on a tape recorder to share with someone else in story time. These stories may be bound in small booklets.

Note: Sentences that can be written in one line of print often require two or more lines in braille. Words should be grouped in meaningful phrases. Never break a phrase at the end of a braille line. Never hyphenate words in the primary grades, until hyphenation has been introduced in their reader. The vocabulary in a reading chart should be controlled so that it corresponds as closely as possible to that found in the reader.

Answering questions with phrases

Children who have had a story read to them by the teacher are given phrases brailled on strips of paper that are placed in front of them on a rubber pad. The student is then asked to find the answer to a question such as, "Where did the little boy go?" The student would be expected to pick out a phrase, such as, "Into the house."

The Rocket Ship

A number is attached to each pocket in a pocket note book. A cut out of the Earth is placed on the front cover, a cut out of the Moon is placed on the back cover. Tell the child that they will take a trip to the moon. They will stop at many space stations along the way. Cut simple rocket shapes out of medium weight cardboard, attach a small pocket to each rocket. Tell the children that each rocket will carry a different payload each day. Payloads may be as follows: (1) Things people can do—sleep in a bed, walk into a house. (2) Things people cannot do—sit in the sky, fly like a bird, swim like a fish. (3) Silly sentences—a cat can fly, gum can jump, Daddy is little.

The BIG Family

Provide concentrated exposure to the same word if it is difficu.t for the student to remember. Tell the student that each sentence that contains the word "big" is a member of the BIG family. Ask the student to read the sentences and locate the one sentence that does not belong to the BIG family.

BIG

The dog is big.
The house is big.
The girls has a big kitten.
The big kitten is yellow.

The big dog is black.
The girl is big.
I see the kitten.

Riddles

A short riddle is brailled onto a 5″ x 8″ card. The answer to the riddle is brailled on another card and taped to the back of the first card, to make the activity self correcting.

Example: I am little. I am grey. I have a long bushy tail. My home is in a tree. I like to eat nuts. What am I? (Answer on the back of the card: I am a Squirrel.)

Comprehension

Select three small dolls to represent three characters from the reader. Place the dolls on the desk in front of the children. Place a milk carton next to each doll. Attach a card which contains the name of the doll to each of the corresponding cartons. Give the student a box containing a number of sentence strips. Ask the student to read each sentence and then put it into the box next to the character who is represented by the action in the sentence.

Example:

Ann	Mark	Mother

made cookies
climbed a tree
has a red dress

Yes or No

Answer the questions by marking Yes or No.

Does a bug have legs?	Yes or no _____
Can a bird fly?	Yes or no _____
Can a rabbit fly like a bird?	Yes or no _____
Can a bird hop like a rabbit?	Yes or no _____

The reading program in the intermediate grades is designed to foster mature reading skills and maintain a high interest in reading. Many students will continue to need help in basic reading skills until the skills are mastered. Other students will be ready to apply their acquired skills for a number of different purposes.

Reference books such as dictionaries and encyclopedias must be made available in braille to the braille user if he is to develop mature and functional braille reading. Countless reading activities and games which may be easily adapted into braille may be found in reading guides designed for use with sighted intermediate grade students. At this level, students often enjoy creating their own games.

Summary and Conclusions

A complete program of reading instruction must include developmental, functional, and recreational reading activities. Traditionally, most programs of reading instruction for the braille users have focused on the developmental and functional reading skills. Means must be found to provide recreational reading activities that reinforce and maintain formally introduced skills and also promote a high level of motivation for learning to read.

To provide a more appropriate reading environment for young braille users, researchers need to collect data relevant to the following questions:

1. Are there skills of braille reading that require specific instruction, not found in the curriculum of the regular classroom?
2. To what extent do braille signs and contractions influence the acquisition of good braille reading skills?
3. Does plastic braille affect the rate and accuracy of the braille reader?
4. During the reading period in the regular classroom, what proportion of time do sighted children spend on recreational reading activities, as defined in this article?
5. During which reading activities in the regular classroom are mainstreamed visually handicapped students most often NOT participating?
6. What kinds of materials must be provided to regular classroom teachers, in order to mainstream visually handicapped students more fully?

References

Burns, Paul C. and Leo M. Schell, *Elementary School Language Arts:* Selected Readings. Chicago: Rand McNally, 1969.

Carter, Homer L. J. and Dorothy J. McGinnis, *Diagnosis and Treatment of the Disabled Reader.* New York: MacMillan, 1970.

Forte, Imogene and Joy MacKenzie, Marjorie Frank. *Kids' Stuff,* Reading and language experiences Intermediate-Junior High. Incentive Publications, Nashville, Tennessee: 1973.

Forte, Imogene and Joy MacKenzie, *Nooks, Crannies, and Corners:* Learning Centers for Creative Classrooms, Nashville, Tennessee: Incentive Publications, 1972.

Heilman, Arthur W. and Elizabeth Ann Holmes, *Smuggling Language Into the Teaching or Reading.* Columbus, Ohio: Charles E. Merrill, 1968.

Huck, Charlotte and Doris Young Kuhn, *Children's Literature in the Elementary School.* New York: Holt, Rinehart, and Winston, 1968.

Mangold, Sally. *Touch and Color.* Castro Valley, CA: Exceptional Teaching Aids, 1980.

Myers, R. E. and E. Paul Torrance, *Can You Imagine?* Boston; Ginn and Company, 1965.

Petty, Walter T. and Mary Bowen, *Slithery Snakes and Other Aids to Children's Writing.* New York: Appleton, Century, Crofts, 1967.

Platts, Mary E. *Spice.* Suggested Activities to Motivate the Teaching of the Primary Language Arts. Stevensville, Michigan: 1973.

Appendix A

Non-factual Questions for Checking Comprehension

Factual questions, more commonly referred to as questions for "literal compehension", are not difficult for teachers to formulate. Below is a list of questions of a non-factual nature that can help teachers individualize reading for their students.

1) What happened in the story that happened to you?
2) How is the life of the main character most like your own life? Least like your life?
3) Have you known people like those in this story?
4) What things that happened in this story would you like to have happen to you?
5) What character in the story would you like to be? Why?
6) How is this book more/less interesting than TV?
7) How did this book make you feel?
8) If you could have changed something about the story, what would it be?
9) Have you read another book similar to this before? How were they alike?
10) What was something in the book you were unable to understand?
11) If this story were being read aloud, what would the audience be like?
12) Did the book teach you a lesson of any kind. If so, what was it?
13) Who else in your class would you recommend read this book?
14) Can you say something good or bad about the book in one sentence?
15) Sometimes we say the opposite from what we mean. Example: Fat people are called "tiny." Did this happen in your book? If so, give an example.
16) Make up another title for your book.
17) Was there any exaggeration in your story?
18) Did any words or sentences the author used make you think of something other than what he was talking about?
19) If you helped someone else get ready to read this book, what would you say?
20) Did anyone in the story speak differently than you or your parents?
21) What could you guess about the characters in this story that is not told about them?
22) What was the author trying to do to you in the book?
23) What kind of experience would a person have to have before he could write a book like this?
24) When some people like or don't like a book, they say things like: It hit me hard"; "It made me sick." Can you use language like this about your book?

Appendix B

Diagnostic Assessment of Braille Reading Skills
Compiled by Rose Marie Swallow, Ed.D.

Name_____ School _____ Grade_____

Teacher _____ Date _____

Note: The braille reading teacher must have:
1. Adequate knowledge of the braille reading code in order to analyse the reading errors of the child.
2. Thorough understanding of the major reading methods in order to match the braille reading approach to the child's reading skills and learning style.
3. Specific skills in adapting and modifying reading strategies based upon the assessed needs of the child.
4. Pertinent information relative to the teaching of braille reading in order to insure proper skills development.

A. Child is able to:

	Yes	No
1. Easily locate		
1.1 Top of page	____	____
1.2 Braille page number	____	____
1.3 Print page number	____	____
1.4 Beginning of each braille line	____	____
1.5 End of each braille line	____	____
2. Position braille book correctly	____	____
3. Track evenly across every page with		
____ two hands	____	____
____ one hand	____	____
3.1 Does not back-track	____	____
3.2 Does not use regressive hand movements	____	____
3.3 Tracks without scrubbing letters	____	____
3.4 Uses light pressure	____	____
4. Correct posture		
4.1 Hands relaxed	____	____
4.2 Fingers curved	____	____
4.3 Sitting		
5. Page turning		
5.1 Turns braille pages easily	____	____
5.2 Reads last line with left hand and turns page with right hand	____	____

B. Finger monitoring
1. Describe fine-motor development.
   1.1 Finger strength:

1.2 Manual dexterity:
1.3 Manipulative behavior:
1.4 Grasp behavior:
1.5 Thumb/index finger opposition:
2. Describe finger sensitivity to braille line.

left   right

2.1 Left hand:
2.2 Right hand:

C. Braille reading type errors
1. Reversals or rotations (circle errors)

c/f	e/i	h/j	m/sh
n/ed	o/ow	p/th	r/w
s/wh	t/ou	z/the	ar/gh
————	————	————	————
ed/the	m/u	s/gh	er/with
————	————	————	————

2. Whole word signs (e.g., can, rather, that, this, which)

————————   ————————   ————————   ————————
————————   ————————   ————————   ————————
————————   ————————   ————————   ————————

3. Short form words (i.e., across, also, good, perhaps, etc.)

————————   ————————   ————————   ————————
————————   ————————   ————————   ————————
————————   ————————   ————————   ————————
————————   ————————   ————————   ————————

4. Two-cell contractions (fill-in errors)
4.1 Initial letters (i.e., day, here, part, right, etc.)

————————   ————————   ————————   ————————
————————   ————————   ————————   ————————

4.2 Final letter contractions (i.e., -sion, -tion, -ation)

————————   ————————   ————————   ————————
————————   ————————   ————————   ————————

5. Confusions
5.1 Letter similarity (i.e., lr h = have, here, his, had)

————————   ————————   ————————   ————————
————————   ————————   ————————   ————————

5.2 Braille position errors (i.e., f, from, ff, !)

_____   _____   _____   _____

_____   _____   _____   _____

_____   _____   _____   _____

5.3 Words with two braille symbols (i.e., to, was, were, his)

_____   _____   _____   _____

_____   _____   _____   _____

_____   _____   _____   _____

D. Word recognition skills (use any good reading skills assessment)
  1. Sight word recognition (i.e., Dolch):
     APH Dolch list _____ percent correct. Date: _____
  2. Phonetic analysis: *Yes*   *No*
     The child is able to —
     2.1 Recognize the following single consonants   _____   _____
         and name a word containing each conso-
         nant.
         (Circle errors)
         b, c, d, f, g, h , j, k, l, m, n,
         p, q, r, s, t, v, w, x, y, and z
     2.2 Recognize a consonant blend and give a
         word containing one of them.
         Example: brick, flower or spring   _____   _____
     2.3 Recognize a consonant digraph and give a
         word containing one of them.
         Example: ship, chain and those   _____   _____
     2.4 Recognize each single vowel and give a
         word containing the long vowel sound.
         Example: a, e, i, o, u, and y   _____   _____
     2.5 Recognize each single vowel and give a
         word containing the short vowel sound.
         Example: a, e, i, o, u, and y   _____   _____
     2.6 Recognize a dipthong and give a word con-
         taining it.
         Example: boy, ouch, and boil   _____   _____
     2.7 Understands how *r* after a vowel affects the
         sound of the vowel.
         Example: her, skirt, and fur   _____   _____
     2.8 Understands how *w* before a vowel affects
         the sound of the vowel.
         Example: wall and worm   _____   _____
     2.9 Understands how a vowel sounds when it is
         followed by *l*.
         Example: ball, doll, and fall   _____   _____
     2.10 Understands the following rules:
          a. When two vowels are together, the first
             is often long and the second is silent.
             Example: tail, fear, and goat   _____   _____

    b. A single vowel in a word or syllable is
      short.
      Example: ran, dot, and sun   _____   _____
    c. A single *e* at the end of a word is silent
      and makes the preceding vowel long.
      Example: rake, date, and tape   _____   _____

3. Structural analysis: *Yes*   *No*
   The child is able to —
   3.1 Recognize a base or root word.
      Example: walks, walked, and walking   _____   _____
   3.2 Understands the function of suffixes.
      Example: s, ed, ing, y, en, and es   _____   _____
              ly, ful, les, ness, er, en   _____   _____
   3.3 Understands the function of prefixes.
      Example: a, un, in, and be,   _____   _____
              b, pro, and re   _____   _____
   3.4 Recognizes the number of syllables in
      words pronounced aloud
            Two syllable words   _____   _____
            Three syllable words   _____   _____
            Four syllable words   _____   _____
   3.5 Applies these rules of syllabication:
      a. A word usually contains as many vowels
        as there are syllables in the word.   _____   _____
      b. When two consonants come between
        vowels, one consonant goes with each
        vowel.
        Example: let/ter   _____   _____
      c. When one consonant comes between two
        vowels, the first syllable usually ends
        with the vowel, and the second syllable
        begins with the second consonant.
        Example: ta/ble   _____   _____
      d. When the first of two vowels separated
        by a single consonant has a short sound,
        the single intervening consonant ends
        the first syllable.
        Example: cam/el   _____   _____
      e. Divides a compound word correctly.
        Example: fire/men, play/ground   _____   _____
      f. Applies the principle of dropping the
        final *e* and adding *ing.*
        Example: raking   _____   _____
      g. Applies the principle of doubling the
        final consonant before adding *ing.*
        Example: running   _____   _____
      h. Applies the principle of changing *y* to *i*
        and adding *es.*

Example: babies

i. Understand contractions.

Example: doesn't

4. Context clue usage:

The child is able to —

	Yes	No
4.1 Decode the braille contractions with limited braille clues. Example: Sally is coming to the car.	___	___
4.2 Apply context clue usage effectively in determining the meaning of an unknown word.	___	___
4.3 Complete a context clue exercise. Example: Mary wants to go for a _____ (red, ride, rake) on a train	___	___

5. Dictionary usage:

The child is able to—

	Yes	No
5.1 Use a braille dictionary to locate the meaning of unknown words.	___	___
5.2 Use a simplified dictionary to locate the pronunciation and meaning of unknown words.	___	___

E. Comprehension skills:

The child is able to:

	Yes	No
1. Answer literal or factual questions which have been asked from stories read.	___	___
2. Answer interpretive questions which are based upon stories read.	___	___
3. Answer questions which require critical or evaluative judgment.	___	___
4. Follow up the reading in a problem-solving situation such as by creative writing, role playing or creative dramatics.	___	___

F. Silent reading:

The child is able to —

	Yes	No
1. Enjoy silent reading.	___	___
2. Maintain proper posture and book position.	___	___
3. Not use lip movement or whispering.	___	___
4. Use proper hand movements while reading silently.	___	___
5. Read at a functional (reasonable) rate.	___	___

G. Oral reading:

The child is able to —

	Yes	No
1. Enjoy oral reading.		
1.1 With the VH teacher	___	___
1.2 In the regular classroom	___	___
2. Read with good oral expession.	___	___
3. Observe punctuation marks while reading orally.	___	___

4. Read in phrases or groups of word.   _____ _____
5. Read with few addition or omission reading
   type errors.   _____ _____
6. Read without repeating words or phrases.   _____ _____

H. Reading rate is _____ wpm.
   Reading comprehension is _____ grade level.

I. Justify reading series or method selected.
   Check
   _____ Sight
   _____ Phonics
   _____ Experiential
   _____ Linguistic
   _____ Multisensory
   State the reasons for selection and relate these to the child's assess-
   ed skills.

   State the reading objectives for _____ year in behavior terms.
   1.

   2.

   3.

   4.

   5.

106

Appendix C
Worksheet Ideas for Developing Braille Tactual Skills

The ideas which follow are excerpts from the Braille Tactual Skills Section of the *Reading Skills Continuum* developed by the staff of the Texas State School for the Blind. The format suggestions are intended for the teacher to braille in the form of worksheets. Students should be given the worksheets prior to any introduction to braille letter recognition.

1) *Format:* Horizontal lines of braille dots (2,5) with regular breaks between them.
   Directions to Student: Track across the lines and verbalize "break" each time a break occurs.
2) *Format:* Same as #1 except with irregular breaks.
   Directions to Student: Same as #1.
3) *Format:* Horizontal dots (1,4) and (3,6).
   Directions to Student: Track across the lines and tell whether the dots are "high" or "low."
4) *Format:* Sames as #3 except intermingle several breaks among the braille characters.
   Directions to Student: Track across the lines and tell whether there is a "high" symbol, "low" symbol, or a break.
5) *Format:* Horizontal lines of dots (1,4) (2,5) and (3,6).
   Directions to Student: Track across the lines and tell whether dots are "high" dots, "low" dots, or "middle" dots.
6) *Format:* Sames as #5 except intermingle several breaks among the braille characters.
   Directions to Student: Track across the lines and tell whether there is a set of "high," "low" or "middle" dots or a break.
7) *Format:* Rows of braille dots (1,3) (4,6), (1,6), and (3,4).
   Directions to Student: Tell whether the dots are "straight up and down" or "slanted."
8) *Format:* Tows of braille dots (1,3) (4,6), (1,2), (2,3), (4,5), and (5,6).
   Directions to Student: Track across the lines and tell whether the dots are "close together" or "far apart."
9) *Format:* Rows of braille dots (1,3), (4,6), (1,2), (2,3), (4,5), (5,6), (1,6), and (3,4).
   Directions to Student: Track across the braille lines and tell whether the dots are "straight up and down-close together." "straight up and down-far apart," or slanted."
10) *Format:* Rows of braille dots (1,6), (1,5), (3,4), (2,4), (3,5), and (2,6).
   Directions to Student: Track across the lines and tell whether the dots are "slanted-close together" or "slanted-far apart."

11) *Format:* Rows of braille dots (1,6), (2,4), (1,5), (5,6), (1,2), (3,5), (2,6), (1,3), (4,6), (1,3), and (3,4).
Directions to Student: Track across the lines and tell whether the dots are "slanted-close together," "slanted-far apart," "straight up and down-close together," or "straight up and down-far apart."

12) *Format:* Rows of braille dots (1,3), (1,6), (2,4), (1,5), (5,6), (1,2), (3,5), (2,3), (4,5), and (2,5).
Directions to Student: Track across the lines and tell whether the dots are "slanted," "straight up and down," or "side by side."

13) *Format:* Rows consisting of two cells followed by a space, with dots 1,2 and 3 in the first cell and some combination of 2 of these three dots in the second cell.
Directions to Student: Track across the lines and tell whether the missing dot in the second cell is a "high," "low," or "middle" dot.

14) *Format:* Rows containing two braille cells followed by a space, in which the first braille cell is a full cell sign, and the second cell contains only 5 dots in various combinations.
Directions to Student: Track across the lines and tell whether the missing dot is on the "right side," "left side," "high," or "low" or "middle."

15) *Format:* Rows of braille cells consisting of various numbers of dots.
Directions to Student: Identify verbally the number of dots in each cell.

16) *Format:* Rows of braille cells arranged in the following order: Full cell, (4,5,6), (1,2,3), full cell.
Directions to Student: Verbally count the number of cells in each row.

Note: The teacher will initially want to double space between the rows of braille characters on the worksheets. Students who are achieving 100 percent accuracy on a particular worksheet may wish to time themselves and record their rate of progress each day.

Appendix D

Index of Materials and Publishing Companies

Materials referred to in the body of this textbook are listed alphabetically and indexed for their availability from publishers. Publishers are given letter codes which are spelled out in full following the list of materials.

Name of Material	Publisher*
Boehm Test of Basic Concepts	APH
Catalog of Tangible Apparatus	APH
Consonant Lotto	GP

Low Vocabulary-High Interest Books
Alby Alligator Series
Animal Adventure Program
Cowboy Sam
Dan Frontier Program
Helicopter Adventure Series
Moonbeam Series — BP
Mystery Adventure Program
Racing Wheels Program
Space Science Fiction
Treat Truck Program

Rock and Pop Stars
Sports Superstars — CWC

Good Literature for the Slow Reader
Re-written Classics — FRC
Special Needs Series

Rock and roll
Sports Superstars
Super Band Champions — PBSC
The Entertainers

Low Vocabulary-High Interest Books
Reader's Digest Skill Builders — ETA
Mangold Developmental Program of Tactile Perception and Braille Letter Recognition
Phonics We Use Learning Games — LC
Raised Line Graph Paper — APH
Raised Line Paper — APH
Speech to Print Phonics — HBJ
SRA Word Games Laboratory — SRA
Teaching Reading through Creative Movement — KIMBO

*See p. 109 for full names and addresses.

Publisher's Index

Letter Code	Name	Address
APH	American Printing House for the Blind	1839 Frankfort Avenue Louisville, Kentucky 40206
BP	Benefit Press	10306 West Roosevelt Road Westchester, Illinois 60153
CWC	Child's World Company	P.O. Box 681 Elgin, Illinois 60120
ETA	Exceptional Teaching Aids	20102 Woodbine Avenue Castro Valley, California 94546
FRC	Frank Richards Company	P.O. Box 66 Phoenix, New York 13135
GP	Garrard Press	Champaign, Illinois 61820
HBJ	Harcourt Brace & Co.	6277 Sea Harbor Drive Orlando, FL 32887
KIMBO	Kimbo Educational Records	Box 55 Deal, New Jersey 07723
LC	Lyons E. Carnahan Educational Publishers Affiliate of Meridith Publishing Company	407 E. 25th Street Chicago, Illinois 60616
PBSC	Paperback Book Supply Co.	1224 West Van Buren Street Chicago, Illinois 60607
SRA	Science Research Associates	259 Erie St. Chicago, Illinois 60611

NOTES

The mission of the American Foundation for the Blind (AFB) is to enable persons who are blind or visually impaired to achieve equality of access and opportunity that will ensure freedom of choice in their lives.